WAY MAKERS

WAY MAKERS

AN ANTHOLOGY
OF WOMEN'S WRITING
ABOUT WALKING

Edited by

KERRI ANDREWS

REAKTION BOOKS

Published by
REAKTION BOOKS LTD
Unit 32, Waterside
44–48 Wharf Road
London N1 7UX, UK
www.reaktionbooks.co.uk

First published 2023
Copyright © Kerri Andrews 2023

Printed and bound in Great Britain
by TJ Books Ltd, Padstow, Cornwall

A catalogue record for this book is available from the British Library

ISBN 978 1 78914 787 2

Contents

To my children, Fhionnlagh and Elisabeth.
May our walks continue to take time,
hold wonder and bring us joy.

For my mother.

Introduction

This book is the first anthology of women's writing about walking. It seems remarkable to be writing that in mid-2022, when anthologies of walking pepper bookshelves in hundreds of bookshops, but it is nonetheless true. The odd woman has occasionally been admitted into the pages of these other anthologies, but only ever in small numbers and often not at all. You might be tempted to observe that few women write about walking, so what did I expect? And I would answer that that hasn't ever been true. We just weren't paying attention.

Some of the material I have gathered for this anthology has lain in archives, accessible only to those who visit in person and know what is there. Most of what I have included, though, has been available in some form or other for a long time. Indeed, much of it has lain in plain sight. It is a mystery to me how anthologies of walking literature have so far missed how essential being on foot is to *Frankenstein*'s terrible, unbearable, denouement. Surely Mary Shelley's imagining of Frankenstein's flight across the world, half pursuing and half pursued, deserves to be recognized as one of the great literary walks. Elizabeth Barrett Browning, writing a little later in the nineteenth century, unforgettably conjures walking as a metaphor for control in a woman's life: the chance to choose to 'walk' whatever path in life a woman might desire is essential, regardless of choices made on a genteel walk of courtship in a chaperoned garden. For Barrett Browning, and indeed for most of the women in this anthology, the ability to determine where our feet go is the ability to decide the path our lives take. Elizabeth Carter knew this when she was writing in the 1740s, and so did the women who followed her, whether they were working as milkwomen in the hills above Bristol, as Ann Yearsley was in the 1780s, or whether they used the power of walking to teach young women how to move through the world, as Frances Burney and Charlotte Smith did.

Walking is, for the women included in this anthology, a source of creativity and comfort; it is a means of expressing grief, longing and desire. It is also a complicated activity: it means freedom, but is also sometimes tinged with danger, as a number of novels of the early twentieth century, by writers including Sylvia Townsend Warner and Dorothy L. Sayers, demonstrate. As well as these literary imaginings of dangerous walks are accounts of walks taken in real life that take strange turns, such as Gwen John's letters about living as an itinerant artist in France, followed and harassed by men as she tramped from place to place. In contrast, Simone de Beauvoir found France the ideal location for discovering a joy in walking, and her accounts of her formative years as a hiker of great confidence with no regard for the conventions of walking groups, or society at large, are thrilling.

As well as walks across clifftops, over mountains and moors, down rivers and glens and through woodland, you will also find in this anthology imaginary walks, fantastical walks, 'unwalks'. Walks of the mind matter as much as walks of the body, with writers such as Gwyneth Lewis and Polly Atkin offering alternative visions of what it means to be afoot, showing us different ways of moving through the world.

And just as women have written, and are writing, about all kinds of walking, they are doing so across form. You will find in this anthology extracts from novels, letters, journals, guidebooks and essays, as well as poetry and the occasional play. Walking as a physical act, a literary device, a spiritual experience, is full of meaning for women, whatever expectations we have been taught to have.

IN BRINGING TOGETHER this selection of writing I have attempted to be inclusive of as many kinds of voice as possible, though there will inevitably be gaps and omissions which deserve to be filled. Some of those gaps will be attributable to the permissions I was able to gain to reproduce more recent material; more of those gaps will be due to my ignorance. I very much hope if you are annoyed by what I've missed you will express your frustration by producing your own anthology of women's writing about walking. I will look forward to buying and reading it. While this might sound facetious I mean it seriously. I have included in this anthology writers from a range of social, racial and bodily backgrounds but I have not managed to move much beyond the Anglophone world. And those writers I *have* included represent a fraction of the material out there that could, and should, reach an audience with a passion for women writing about walking, adventuring, being outdoors, and imagining worlds through walking. There is plenty more work to be done if we are to properly acknowledge and celebrate the full range of what women have written about walking, and how they have used it as a creative tool, a way of moving through this world and beyond it.

This anthology is a start. May it not be the end.

Elizabeth Carter to
Catherine Talbot, 1746

As you desire a full and true account of my whole life and conversation, it is necessary in the first place you should be made acquainted with the singular contrivance by which I am called in the morning. There is a bell placed at the head of my bed, and to this is fastened a packthread and a piece of lead, which, when I am not lulled by the soft zephyrs through the broken pane, is conveyed through a crevasse of my window into a garden below, pertaining to the Sexton, who gets up between four and five, and pulls the said packthread with as much heart and good-will as if he was ringing my knell. By this most curious invention I make a shift to get up, which I am too stupid to do without calling. Some evil-minded people of my acquaintance have most wickedly threatened to cut my bell-rope, which would be the utter undoing of me; for I should infallibly sleep out the whole summer. And now I am up, you may belike enquire to what purpose. I sit down to my several lessons as regular as a school-boy, and lay in a stock of learning to make a figure with at breakfast; but for this I am not ready. My general practice about six is to take up my stick and walk, sometimes alone, and at others with a companion, whom I call in my way, and draw out half asleep, and consequently incapable of reflecting on the danger of such an undertaking; for to be sure she might just as well trust herself to the guidance of a jack-a-lanthorn: however, she has the extreme consolation of grumbling as much as she pleases without the least interruption, which she does with such a variety of comical phrases, that I generally laugh from the beginning to the end of our journey. I must make you a little acquainted with her, by telling you it was she who versified the proclamation of the immortal John Redman of Walmer. Many are the exercises of patience she meets with in our peregrination, sometimes half roasted with the full glare of sunshine upon an open common, then dragged through a thread-paper path in the middle of a cornfield, and bathed up to the ears in dew, and at the end of it perhaps forced to scratch her way through the bushes of a close shady lane, never before frequented by any animal but birds. In short, towards the conclusion of our walk, we make such deplorable ragged figures, that I wonder some prudent country justice does not take us up for vagrants, and cramp our rambling genius in the stocks. An apprehension that does not half so much fright me, as when some civil swains pull off their hats, and I hear them signifying to one another, with a note of admiration, that *I am Parson Carter's daughter*. I had much rather be accosted with 'good morrow, sweet-heart,' or 'are you walking for a wager.'

Frances Burney,
Evelina; or, The History of a Young Lady's Entrance into the World (1778)

Letter XLVI

Holborn, June 17th.

Yesterday Mr. Smith carried his point, of making a party for Vauxhall, consisting of Madame Duval, M. Du Bois, all the Branghtons, Mr. Brown, himself, – and me! – for I find all endeavours vain to escape any thing which these people desire I should not.

There were twenty disputes previous to our setting out; first, as to the *time* of our going: Mr Branghton, his son, and young Brown, were for six o'clock; and all the ladies and Mr. Smith were for eight; – the latter, however, conquered.

Then, as to the *way* we should go; some were for a boat, others for a coach, and Mr. Branghton himself was for walking; but the boat, at length, was decided upon. Indeed this was the only part of the expedition that was agreeable to me, for the Thames was delightfully pleasant.

The Garden is very pretty, but too formal; I should have been better pleased, had it consisted less of straight walks, where

Grove nods at grove, each alley has its brother.

The trees, the numerous lights, and the company in the circle around the orchestra make a most brilliant and gay appearance; and, had I been with a party less disagreeable to me, I should have thought it a place formed for animation and pleasure. There was a concert, in the course of which a hautbois concerto was so charmingly played, that I could have thought myself upon enchanted ground, had I had spirits more gentle to associate with. The hautbois in the open air is heavenly.

Mr. Smith endeavoured to attach himself to me, with such officious assiduity and impertinent freedom, that he quite sickened me. Indeed, M. Du Bois was the only man of the party to whom, voluntarily, I ever addressed myself. He is civil and respectful, and I have found nobody else so since I left Howard Grove. His English is very bad; but I prefer it to speaking French myself, which I dare not venture to do. I converse with him frequently, both to disengage myself from others, and to oblige Madame Duval, who is always pleased when he is attended to.

As we were walking about the orchestra, I heard a bell ring, and, in a moment, Mr. Smith, flying up to me, caught my hand, and, with a motion too quick to be resisted, ran away with me many yards before I had breath to ask his meaning, though I struggled as well as I could, to get from him. At last, however, I insisted upon stopping: 'Stopping, Ma'am!' cried he, 'why we must run on, or we shall lose the cascade!'

And then again, he hurried me away, mixing with a crowd of people, all running with so much velocity, that I could not imagine what had raised such an alarm. We were soon followed by the rest of the party; and my surprise and ignorance proved a source of diversion to them all, that was not exhausted the whole evening. Young Branghton, in particular, laughed till he could hardly stand.

The scene of the cascade I thought extremely pretty, and the general effect striking and lively.

But this was not the only surprise which was to divert them at my expense; for they led me about the garden, purposely to enjoy my first sight of various other deceptions.

About ten o'clock, Mr. Smith having chosen a *box* in a very conspicuous place, we all went to supper. Much fault was found with every thing that was ordered, though not a morsel of any thing was left; and the dearness of the provisions, with conjectures upon what profit was made by them, supplied discourse during the whole meal.

When wine and cyder were brought, Mr. Smith said, 'Now let's enjoy ourselves; now is the time, or never. Well, Ma'am, and how do you like Vauxhall?'

'Like it!' cried young Branghton, 'why, how can she help liking it? she has never seen such a place before, that I'll answer for.'

'For my part,' said Miss Branghton, 'I like it because it is not vulgar.'

'This must have been a fine treat for you, Miss,' said Mr. Branghton; 'why, I suppose, you was never so happy in all your life before?'

I endeavoured to express my satisfaction with some pleasure, yet I believe they were much amazed at my coldness.

'Miss ought to stay in town till the last night,' said young Branghton; 'and then, it's my belief, she'd say something to it! Why, Lord, it's the best night of any; there's always a riot, – and there the folks run about, – and then there's such squealing and squalling! – and there all the lamps are broke, – and the women run skimper scamper; – I declare I would not take five guineas to miss the last night!'

I was very glad when they all grew tired of sitting, and called for the waiter to pay the bill. The Miss Branghtons said they would walk on, while the gentlemen settled the account, and asked me to accompany them; which, however, I declined.

'You girls may do as you please,' said Madame Duval; 'but as to me, I promise you, I sha'n't go no where without the gentlemen.'

'No more, I suppose, will my *Cousin*,' said Miss Branghton, looking reproachfully towards Mr. Smith.

This reflection, which I feared, would flatter his vanity, made me, most unfortunately, request Madame Duval's permission to attend them. She granted it, and away we went, having promised to meet in the room.

To the room, therefore, I would immediately have gone: but the sisters agreed that they would first have a *little pleasure*, and they tittered, and talked so loud, that they attracted universal notice.

'Lord, Polly,' said the eldest, 'suppose we were to take a turn in the dark walks!'

'Aye, do,' answered she, 'and then we'll hide ourselves, and then Mr. Brown will think we are lost.'

I remonstrated very warmly against this plan, telling them that it would endanger our missing the rest of the party all the evening.

'O dear,' cried Miss Branghton, 'I thought how uneasy Miss would be without a beau!'

This impertinence I did not think worth answering; and, quite by compulsion, I followed them down a long alley, in which there was hardly any light.

By the time we came near the end, a large party of gentlemen, apparently very riotous, and who were hallooing, leaning on one another, and laughing immoderately, seemed to rush suddenly from behind some trees, and meeting us face to face, put their arms at their sides, and formed a kind of circle, that first stopped our proceeding, and then our retreating, for we were presently entirely inclosed. The Miss Branghtons screamed aloud, and I was frightened exceedingly; our screams were answered with bursts of laughter, and for some minutes, we were kept prisoners, till at last one of them, rudely, seizing hold of me, said I was a pretty little creature.

Terrified to death, I struggled with such vehemence to disengage myself from him, that I succeeded, in spite of his efforts to detain me; and immediately, and with a swiftness which fear only could have given me, I flew rather than ran up the walk, hoping to secure my safety by returning to the lights and company we had so foolishly left: but before I could possibly accomplish my purpose, I was met by another party of men, one of whom placed himself so directly in my way, calling out, 'Whither so fast, my love?' – that I could only have proceeded, by running into his arms.

In a moment both my hands, by different persons, were caught hold of; and one of them, in a most familiar manner, desired to accompany me in a race, when I ran next; while the rest of the party stood still and laughed.

I was almost distracted with terror, and so breathless with running, that I could not speak, till another advancing, said, I was as handsome as an angel, and desired to be of the party. I then just articulated, 'For Heaven's sake, gentlemen, let me pass!'

Another then, rushing suddenly forward, exclaimed, 'Heaven and earth! What voice is that? – '

'The voice of the prettiest little actress I have seen this age,' answered one of my persecutors.

'No, – no, – no – ' I *panted* out, 'I am no actress – pray let me go, – pray let me pass –'

'By all that's sacred,' cried the same voice, which I then knew for Sir Clement Willoughby's, ''tis herself!'

'Sir Clement Willoughby!' cried I. 'O, Sir, assist – assist me – or I shall die with terror!'

'Gentlemen,' cried he, disengaging them all from me in an instant, 'pray leave this lady to me.'

Loud laughs proceeded from every mouth, and two or three said, '*Willoughby has all the luck!*' But one of them, in a passionate manner, vowed he would not give me up, for that he had the first right to me, and would support it.

'You are mistaken,' said Sir Clement, 'this lady is – I will explain myself to you another time; but, I assure you, you are all mistaken.'

And then, taking my willing hand, he led me off, amidst the loud acclamations, laughter, and gross merriment of his impertinent companions.

As soon as we had escaped from them, Sir Clement, with a voice of surprise, exclaimed, 'My dearest creature, what wonder, what strange revolution, has brought you to such a place as this?'

Ashamed of my situation, and extremely mortified to be thus recognized by him, I was for some time silent, and when he repeated his question, only stammered out, 'I have, – I hardly know how, – lost myself from my party –'

He caught my hand, and eagerly pressing it, in a passionate voice said, 'O that I had sooner met with thee!'

Surprised at a freedom so unexpected, I angrily broke from him, saying, 'Is this the protection you give me, Sir Clement?'

And then I saw what the perturbation of my mind had prevented my sooner noticing, that he had led me, though I know not how, into another of the dark alleys, instead of the place whither I meant to go.

'Good God!' I cried, 'where am I? – What way are you going?'

'Where,' answered he, 'we shall be least observed!'

Astonished at this speech, I stopped short, and declared I would go no further.

'And why not, my angel?' again endeavouring to take my hand.

My heart beat with resentment; I pushed him away from me with all my strength, and demanded how he dared treat me with such insolence?

'Insolence!' repeated he.

'Yes, Sir Clement, *insolence*; from you, who know me, I had a claim for protection, – not to such treatment as this.'

'By Heaven,' cried he with warmth, 'you distract me, – why, tell me, – why do I see you here? – Is this a place for Miss Anville? – these dark walks! – no party! no companion! – by all that's good, I can scarce believe my senses!'

Extremely offended at this speech, I turned angrily from him, and, not deigning to make any answer, walked on towards that part of the garden whence I perceived the lights and company.

He followed me; but we were both some time silent.

'So you will not explain to me your situation?' said he, at length.

'No, Sir,' answered I, disdainfully.

'Nor yet – suffer me to make my own interpretation? – '

I could not bear this strange manner of speaking; it made my very soul shudder, – and I burst into tears.

He flew to me, and actually flung himself at my feet, as if regardless who might see him, saying, 'O Miss Anville – loveliest of women – forgive my – my – I beseech you forgive me; – if I have offended, – if I have hurt you I could kill myself at the thought! – '

'No matter, Sir, no matter,' cried I; 'if I can but find my friends, – I will never speak to – never see you again!'

'Good God! – good Heaven! – my dearest life, what is it I have done? – What is it I have said?'

'You best know, Sir, *what* and *why*: – but don't hold me here, – let me be gone; and do *you*!'

'Not till you forgive me! – I cannot part with you in anger.'

'For shame, for shame, Sir!' cried I indignantly, 'do you suppose I am to be thus compelled? – do you take advantage of the absence of my friends, to affront me?'

'No, Madam,' cried he, rising: 'I would sooner forfeit my life than act so mean a part. But you have flung me into amazement unspeakable, and you will not condescend to listen to my request of giving me some explanation.'

'The manner, Sir,' said I, 'in which you spoke that request, made and will make me scorn to answer it.'

'Scorn! – I will own to you, I expected not such displeasure from Miss Anville.'

'Perhaps, Sir, if you had, you would less voluntarily have merited it.'

'My dearest life, surely it must be known to you, that the man does not breathe who adores you so passionately, so fervently, so tenderly as I do! – why then will you delight in perplexing me? – in keeping me in suspense? – in torturing me with doubt?'

'I, Sir, delight in perplexing you! – you are much mistaken. – Your suspense, your doubts, your perplexities, – are of your own creating; and, believe me, Sir, they may *offend* but they can never *delight* me: – but as you have yourself raised, you must yourself satisfy them.'

'Good God! – that such haughtiness and such sweetness can inhabit the same mansion!'

I made no answer; but quickening my pace I walked on silently and sullenly, till this most impetuous of men, snatching my hand, which he grasped with violence, besought me to forgive him with such earnestness of supplication, that, merely to escape his importunities, I was forced to speak, and in some measure to grant the pardon he requested: though it was accorded with a very ill grace; but, indeed, I knew not how to resist the humility of his intreaties: yet never shall I recollect the occasion he gave me of displeasure, without feeling it renewed.

We now soon arrived in the midst of the general crowd, and, my own safety being then insured, I grew extremely uneasy for the Miss Branghtons, whose danger, however imprudently incurred by their own folly, I too well knew how to tremble for. To this consideration all my pride of heart yielded, and I determined to seek my party with the utmost speed; though not without a sigh did I recollect the fruitless attempt I had made, after the opera, of concealing from this man my unfortunate connections, which I was now obliged to make known.

Ann Yearsley, 'Clifton Hill', from *Selected Poems* (1785)

In this lone hour, when angry storms descend,
And the chill'd soul deplores her distant friend;
When all her sprightly fires inactive lie,
And objects fill the mental eye;
When hoary Winter strides the northern blast,
And Flora's beauties at his feet are cast;
Earth by the grisly tyrant desert made,
The feather'd warblers quit the leafless shade;
Quit those dear scenes where life and love began,
And, cheerless, seek the savage haunt of man;
How mourns each tenant of the silent grove!
No soft sensation tunes the heart to love;
No fluttering pulse awakes to Rapture's call;
No strain responsive aids the water's fall.
The Swain neglects his Nymph, yet knows not why;
The Nymph, indifferent, mourns the freezing sky;
Alike insensible to soft desire,
She asks no warmth – but from the kitchen fire;
Love seeks a milder zone; half sunk in snow,
Lactilla, shivering, tends her fav'rite cow;
The bleating flocks now ask the bounteous hand,

And chrystal streams in frozen fetters stand.
The beauteous red-breast, tender in her frame,
Whose murder marks the fool with treble shame,
Near the low cottage door, in pensive mood,
Complains, and mourns her brothers of the wood.
Her song oft wak'd the soul to gentle joys,
All but his ruthless soul whose gun destroys.
For this, rough clown, long pains on thee shall wait,
And freezing want avenge their hapless fate;
For these fell murders may'st thou change thy kind,
In outward form as savage as in mind;
Go, be a bear of Pythagorean name,
From man distinguish'd by thy hideous frame.

Tho' slow and pensive now the moments roll,
Successive months shall from our torpid soul
Hurry these scenes again; the laughing hours
Advancing swift, shall strew spontaneous flowers;
The early-peeping snowdrop, crocus mild,
And modest violet, grace the secret wild;
Pale primrose, daisy, maypole-decking sweet,
And purple hyacinth together meet:
All Nature's sweets in joyous circle move,
And wake the frozen soul again to love.

The ruddy swain now stalks along the vale,
And snuffs fresh ardour from the flying gale;
The landscape rushes on his untaught mind,
Strong raptures rise, but raptures undefin'd;
He louder whistles, stretches o'er the green,

By screaming milk-maids, not unheeded, seen;
The downcast look ne'er fixes on the swain,
They dread his eye, retire and gaze again.
'Tis mighty Love – Ye blooming maids, beware,
Nor the lone thicket with a lover dare.
No high romantic rules of honour bind
The timid virgin of the rural kind;
No conquest of the passions e'er was taught,
No meed e'er given them for the vanquish'd thought.
To sacrifice, to govern, to restrain,
Or to extinguish, or to hug the pain,
Was never theirs; instead, the fear of shame
Proves a strong bulwark, and secures their fame;
Shielded by this, they flout, reject, deny,
With mock disdain put the fond lover by;
Unreal scorn, stern looks, affected pride,
Awe the poor swain, and save the trembling bride.
As o'er the upland hills I take my way,
My eyes in transport boundless scenes survey:
Here the neat dome where sacred raptures rise,
From whence the contrite groan shall pierce the skies;
Where sin-struck souls bend low in humble prayer,
And waft that sigh which ne'er is lost in air.

Ah! sacred turf! here a fond Parent lies,
How my soul melts while dreadful scenes arise!
The past! Ah! shield me, Mercy! from that thought,
My aching brain now whirls, with horror fraught.
Dead! can it be? 'twas here we frequent stray'd,
And these sad records mournfully survey'd.

I mark'd the verse, the skulls her eye invite,
Whilst my young bosom shudder'd with affright!
My heart recoil'd, and shun'd the loathsome view;
'Start not, my child, each human thought subdue,'
She calmly said; 'this fate shall once be thine,
My woes pronounce that it shall first be mine.'
Abash'd, I caught the awful truths she sung,
And on her firm resolves one moment hung;
Vain boast – my bulwark tumbles to the deep,
Amaz'd – alone I climb the craggy steep;
My shrieking soul deserted, sullen views
The depths below, and Hope's fond strains refuse;
I listen'd not – She louder struck the lyre,
And love divine, and moral truths conspire.

The proud Crœsean Crew, light, cruel, vain,
Whose deeds have never swell'd the Muses' strain,
Whose bosoms others sorrows ne'er assail,
Who hear, unheeding, Misery's bitter tale,
Here call for satire, would the verse avail.
Rest, impious race! – The Muse pursues her flight,
Breathes purer air on Vincent's rugged height;
Here nibbling flocks of scanty herbage gain
A meal penurious from the barren plain;
Crop the low niggard bush; and, patient, try
The distant walk, and every hillock nigh:
Some bask, some bound, nor terrors ever know,
Save from the human form, their only foe.
Ye bleating innocents! dispel your fears,
My woe-struck soul in all your troubles shares;

'Tis but Lactilla – fly not from the green:
Long have I shar'd with you this guiltless scene.
'Tis mine to wander o'er the dewy lawn,
And mark the pallid streak of early dawn;
Lo! the grey dusk that fill'd the vacant space,
Now fleets, and infant light pursues the chace;
From the hill top it seeks the valley low;
Inflam'd, the cheeks of morn with blushes glow;
Behold it 'whelmed in a bright flood of day,
It strives no more, but to the God gives way.

Ye silent, solemn, strong, stupendous heights,
Whose terror-striking frown the school-boy frights
From the young daw; whilst in your rugged breast
The chattering brood, secured by Horror, rest.
Say, Muse, what arm the low'ring brothers cleft,
And the calm stream in this low cradle left?
Coëval with Creation they look down,
And, sunder'd, still retain their native frown.
Beneath those heights, lo! balmy springs arise,
To which pale Beauty's faded image flies;
Their kindly powers life's genial heat restore,
The tardy pulse, whose throbs were almost o'er,
Here beats a livelier tune. The breezy air,
To the wild hills invites the languid fair:
Fear not the western gale, thou tim'rous maid,
Nor dread its blast shall thy soft form invade;
Tho' cool and strong the quick'ning breezes blow,
And meet thy panting breath, 'twill quickly grow

More strong; then drink the odoriferous draught,
With unseen particles of health 'tis fraught.
Sit not within the threshold of Despair,
Nor plead a weakness fatal to the fair;
Soft term for INDOLENCE, politely given,
By which we win no joy from earth or heaven.
Foul Fiend! thou bane of health, fair Virtue's bane,
Death of true pleasure, source of real pain!
Keen exercise shall brace the fainting soul,
And bid her slacken'd powers more vigorous roll.

Blame not my rustic lay, nor think me rude,
If I avow Conceit's the grand prelude
To dire disease and death. Your high-born maid,
Whom fashion guides, in youth's first bloom shall fade;
She seeks the cause, th' effect would fain elude,
By Death's o'erstretching stride too close pursu'd,
She faints within his icy grasp, yet stares,
And wonders why the Tyrant yet appears –
Abrupt – so soon – Thine, Fashion is the crime,
Fell Dissipation does the work of time.

How thickly cloath'd, yon rock of scanty soil,
Its lovely verdure scorns the hand of Toil.
Here the deep green, and here the lively plays,
The russet birch, and ever-blooming bays;
The vengeful black-thorn, of wild beauties proud,
Blooms beauteous in the gloomy-chequer'd crowd:
The barren elm, the useful feeding oak,

Whose hamadryad ne'er should feel the stroke
Of axe relentless, 'till twice fifty years
Have crown'd her woodland joys, and fruitful cares.

The pois'nous reptiles here their mischiefs bring,
And thro' the helpless sleeper dart the sting;
The toad envenom'd, hating human eyes,
Here springs to light, lives long, and aged dies.
The harmless snail, slow-journeying, creeps away,
Sucks the young dew, but shuns the bolder day.
(Alas! if transmigration should prevail,
I fear LACTILLA's soul must house in snail.)
The long-nosed mouse, the woodland rat is here,
The sightless mole, with nicely-pointed ear;
The timid rabbit hails th' impervious gloom,
Eludes the dog's keen scent, and shuns her doom.

Various the tenants of this tangled wood,
Who skulk all day, all night review the flood,
Chew the wash'd weed driven by the beating wave,
Or feast on dreadful food, which hop'd a milder grave.
Hail! useful channel! Commerce spreads her wings,
From either pole her various treasure brings;
Wafted by thee, the mariner long stray'd,
Clasps the fond parent, and the sighing maid;
Joy tunes the cry; the rocks rebound the roar,
The deep vibration quivers 'long the shore;
The merchant hears, and hails the peeping mast,
The wave-drench'd sailor scorns all peril past;
Now love and joy the noisy crew invite,

And clumsy music crowns the rough delight.
Yours be the vulgar dissonance, while I
Cross the low stream, and stretch the ardent eye,
O'er Nature's wilds; 'tis peace, 'tis joy serene,
The thought as pure as calm the vernal scene.
Ah, lovely meads! my bosom lighter grows,
Shakes off her huge oppressive weight of woes,
And swells in guiltless rapture; ever hail,
The tufted grove, and the low-winding vale!

Low not, ye herds, your lusty Masters bring
The crop of Summer; and the genial Spring
Feels for your wants, and softens Winter's rage,
The hoarded hay-stack shall your woes assuage;
Woes summ'd in one alone, 'tis Nature's call,
That secret voice which fills creation all.

Beneath this stack Louisa's dwelling rose,
Here the fair Maniac bore three Winters snows.
Here long she shiver'd, stiffening in the blast,
The lightnings round their livid horrors cast;
The thunders roar, while rushing torrents pour,
And add new woes to bleak affliction's hour;
The heavens lour dismal while the storm descends,
No Mother's bosom the soft maid befriends;
But, frighten'd, o'er the wilds she swiftly flies,
And drench'd with rains, the roofless hay-stack tries.
The morn was fair, and gentle – sought
These lonely woodlands, friends to sober Thought;
With Solitude, the slow-pac'd maid is seen

Tread the dark grove, and unfrequented green,
Well – knew their lurkings; Phoebus shone,
While, musing, she pursued the track alone.
O, thou kind friend! whom here I dare not name,
Who to Louisa's shed of misery came,
Lur'd by the tale, sigh'd o'er her beauteous form,
And gently drew her from the beating storm,
Stand forth – defend, for well thou canst, the cause
Of Heaven, and justify its rigid laws;
Yet own that human laws are harshly given,
When they extend beyond the will of Heaven.
Say, can thy pen for that hard duty plead,
By which the meek and helpless maid's decreed
To dire seclusion? Snatch'd from guiltless joys,
To where corroding grief the frame destroys;
Monastic glooms, which active virtue cramp,
Where horrid silence chills the vital lamp;
Slowly and faint the languid pulses beat,
And the chill'd heart forgets its genial heat;
The dim sunk eye, with hopeless glance, explores
The solemn aisles, and death-denouncing doors,
Ne'er to be past again. – Now heaves the sigh,
Now unavailing sorrows fill the eye:
Fancy once more brings back the long-lost youth
To the fond soul, in all the charms of Truth;
She welcomes the lov'd image; busy Thought
Pourtrays the past, with guiltless pleasures fraught;
'Tis momentary bliss, 'tis rapture high,
The heart o'erflows, and all is extacy.
Memory! I charge thee yet preserve the shade,

Ah! let not yet the glittering colours fade!
Forbear the cruel future yet to view,
When the sad soul must bid a long adieu,
E'en to its fancied bliss – Ah! turn not yet
Thou wretched bankrupt, that must soon forget
This farewel draught of joy: lo! Fancy dies,
E'en the thin phantom of past pleasure flies.
Thought sinks in real woe; too poor to give
Her present bliss, she bids the future live;
The spirit soon quits that fond clasp, for see,
The future offers finish'd misery.
Hope quite extinct, lo! frantic thro' the aisles
She raves, while Superstition grimly smiles.
Th' exhausted mourner mopes, then wildly stalks
Round the drear dome, and seeks the darkest walks.
The glance distracted each sad sister meets,
The sorrow-speaking eye in silence greets
Each death-devoted maid; Louisa here
Runs thro' each various shape of sad despair;
Now swells with gusts of hope, now sick'ning dies;
Alternate thoughts of death and life arise
Within her panting soul; the firm resolve,
The new desire, in stronger fears dissolve.
She starts – then seiz'd the moment of her fate,
Quits the lone cloyster and the horrid grate,
Whilst wilder horrors to receive her wait;
Muffled, on Freedom's happy plains they stand,
And eager seize her not reluctant hand;
Too late to these mild shores the mourner came,
For now the guilt of flight o'erwhelms her frame:

Her broken vows in wild disorder roll,
And stick like serpents in her trembling soul;
Thought, what art thou? of thee she boasts no more,
O'erwhelm'd, thou dy'st amid the wilder roar
Of lawless anarchy, which sweeps the soul,
Whilst her drown'd faculties like pebbles roll,
Unloos'd, uptorn, by whirlwinds of despair,
Each well-taught moral now dissolves in air;
Dishevel'd, lo! her beauteous tresses fly,
And the wild glance now fills the staring eye;
The balls, fierce glaring in their orbits move,
Bright spheres, where beam'd the sparkling fires of Love,
Now roam for objects which once fill'd her mind,
Ah! long-lost objects they must never find.
Ill starr'd LOUISA! Memory, 'tis a strain,
Which fills my soul with sympathetic pain.
Remembrance, hence, give thy vain struggles o'er,
Nor swell the line with forms that live no more.

Helen Maria Williams, *Letters Written in France, in the Summer 1790* (1790)

LETTER VIII.

You have not heard, perhaps, that on the day of the Federation at Paris, the national oath was taken throughout the whole kingdom, at the hour of twelve.

A great number of farmers and peasants walked in the procession at Rouen, bearing in their hands the instruments of their husbandry, decorated with national ribbons. The national guard cut down branches from the trees, and stuck them in their hats; and a French gentleman of my acquaintance, who understands English, and reads Shakespeare, told me, that it seemed like Birnham Wood coming to Dunsinane.

The leaders of the French revolution, are men well acquainted with the human heart. They have not trusted merely to the force of reason, but have studied to interest in their cause the most powerful passions of human nature, by the appointment of solemnities perfectly calculated to awaken that general sympathy which is caught from heart to heart with irresistible energy, fills every eye with tears, and throbs in every bosom.

I have heard of a procession, which took place not long ago in one of the districts of Paris, in which five hundred young ladies walked dressed in white, and decorated with cockades of the national ribbon, leading by silken cords a number of prisoners newly released from captivity; and who, with their faces covered by long flowing veils, were conducted to a church, where they returned thanks for their deliverance.

Charlotte Smith, *Rural Walks: In Dialogues: Intended for the Use of Young Persons* (1795)

DIALOGUE XI.
The Alarm.

The dark and gloomy month of November was now arrived; but to outward appearances the family of Mrs. Woodfield gave less attention than usual, for they expected, by every post, to hear that Colonel Cecil, who was arrived in London and slowly recovering, would fix the day for setting out for their abode; and only his earnest desire, and the necessity of constant attendance on her family, prevented his sister from attending him in town.

Every morning, however, when the weather did not forbid their excursions, his daughter and her two cousins went early to the place where the letters were usually left, about a mile and a half from the house, eager to procure some new intelligence of his intended arrival, though Caroline could not think of the approaching interview, which could not fail of being extremely afflicting to them both. When her father bade her adieu, her mother was suffering under a lingering illness, which soon after terminated in her death. The recollection of that scene, as well as of all the dangers her father had since encountered, must make their meeting now very affecting to them both.

The country, which once appeared so melancholy a residence, had now lost its horrors. Gratitude towards her aunt, affection for her cousins, and a taste for the domestic amusements and resources the country afforded, had taken place of that sullen apathy, which, on her coming to reside in the family, had given her aunt so much uneasiness.

The good sense and taste that nature had given her, had now room to display itself; and even the dull and grey skies, the almost dismantled woods, and cheerless aspect, which every object wore around her, failed not to awaken in her mind poetical recollections.

On their way to the cottage by the high road side, which served as a sort of post-house to the neighbouring villages, was a rocky eminence: From the top it afforded a view of the sea; at its foot ran the narrow-winding path; and its abrupt and rugged sides presented, in some places, bare scars of rock, where the sand-martin or the bat had found shelter; in others it was shaded with broom, female fern, and festoons of ivy. It was here that during the heats of summer, the little party had often stopped on their walk, to enjoy the cool shade of the rocks, and the refreshing echoes of the stream that, issuing from a cavern near the top, fell in small but clear and brilliant gushes of water, till it wound away near the path over a deep worn channel, and found its way to the river which crossed a neighbouring heath.

No flowers now adorned its stony acclivity. An old oak, whose tawny leaves had yet resisted the sharp winds of autumn, seemed to mourn over the withered foliage beneath. The three girls stopped a moment, at the desire of Caroline; who, resting upon a fragment of rock recollected that she had somewhere read a description of scenery extremely resembling the landscape before her. A little consideration brought the passage to her mind; but she felt grateful that the last lines had no allusion to her circumstance, who might, from the loss of a father, have found them but too applicable:

'Twas here, even here, where now I sit reclin'd,
And Winter's sighs sound hollow in the wind;
Loud and more loud the blast of Evening raves,
And strips the oaks of their last lingering leaves.
The eddying foliage in the tempest flies,
And fills, with duskier gloom, the thickening skies,
Red sinks the Sun behind the howling hill,
And rushes, with hoarse stream, the mountain rill;
And now, with ruffling billow cold and pale,
Runs, swoln and dashing, down the lonely vale;
While to these tearful eyes, grief's faded form
Sits on the cloud, and sighs amid the storm.'

Hardly had Caroline finished repeating these lines, which, except the hour of the day gave to her imagination the reflection of the scene before her, when suddenly, from an excavation in the rock which had concealed them, came forward a group of gypsies, two men, three women, and several little ragged children, who all speaking together in language peculiar to themselves, began to beg; while the three girls, extremely terrified, walked on as quick as they could, searching, however, for whatever halfpence or small money they had about them, which they threw towards the importunate group; one woman, however, still continuing to follow them, and insisting on being allowed to tell their fortunes, while, on looking back, they saw the two men still gazing after them; their terror, and of course their speed increased, and they at length gained an open road, and saw two men at plough in a field immediately near it. Their troublesome follower then left them, but Caroline though she had more courage than either of her cousins, was so much alarmed at an encounter, which in all their solitary walks had never happened before, that she engaged a farmer's servant whom she met, and whom they happened to know, to attend them for the rest of their walk, and she determined to go home another way.

Mary Wollstonecraft to William Godwin, 10 September 1796

I shall come to you to night, probably, before nine – May I ask you to be at home – I may be tired and not like to ramble further – Should I be later – you will forgive me – It will not be my heart that will loiter – By the bye – I do not tell *any* body – especially yourself – it is always on my lips at your door –

The return of the fine weather has led me to form a vague wish that we might *vagabondize* one day in the country – before the summer is clear gone. I love the country and like to leave certain associations in my memory, which seem, as it were, the land marks of affection – Am I very obscure?

Dorothy Wordsworth,
The Alfoxden Journal (1798)

Alfoxden, 20th January 1798. The green paths down the hill-sides are channels for streams. The young wheat is streaked by silver lines of water running between the ridges, the sheep are gathered together on the slopes. After the wet dark days, the country seems more populous. It peoples itself in the sunbeams. The garden, mimic of spring, is gay with flowers. The purple-starred hepatica spreads itself in the sun, and the clustering snow-drops put forth their white heads, at first upright, ribbed with green, and like a rosebud when completely opened, hanging their heads downwards, but slowly lengthening their slender stems. The slanting woods of an unvarying brown, showing the light through the thin net-work of their upper boughs. Upon the highest ridge of that round hill covered with planted oaks, the shafts of the trees show in the light like the columns of a ruin.

21st. Walked on the hill-tops – a warm day. Sate under the firs in the park. The tops of the beeches of a brown-red or crimson; those oaks fanned by the sea breeze thick with feathery sea-green moss, as a grove not stripped of its leaves. Moss cups more proper than acorns for fairy goblets.

22nd. Walked through the wood to Holford. The ivy twisting round the oaks like bristled serpents. The day cold

– a warm shelter in the hollies, capriciously bearing berries. Query: Are the male and female flowers on separate trees?

23rd. Bright sunshine, went out at 3 o'clock. The sea perfectly calm blue, streaked with deeper colour by the clouds, and tongues or points of sand; on our return of a gloomy red. The sun gone down. The crescent moon, Jupiter, and Venus. The sound of the sea distinctly heard on the tops of the hills, which we could never hear in summer. We attribute this partly to the bareness of the trees, but chiefly to the absence of the singing of birds, the hum of insects, that noiseless noise which lives in the summer air. The villages marked out by beautiful beds of smoke. The turf fading into the mountain road. The scarlet flowers of the moss.

24th. Walked between half-past three and half-past five. The evening cold and clear. The sea of a sober grey, streaked by the deeper grey clouds. The half dead sound of the near sheep-bell, in the hollow of the sloping coombe, exquisitely soothing.

25th. Went to Poole's after tea. The sky spread over with one continuous cloud, whitened by the light of the moon, which, though her dim shape was seen, did not throw forth so strong a light as to chequer the earth with shadows. At once the clouds seemed to cleave asunder, and left her in the centre of a black-blue vault. She sailed along, followed by multitudes of stars, small, and bright, and sharp. Their brightness seemed concentrated, (half-moon).

26th. Walked upon the hill-tops; followed the sheep tracks till we overlooked the larger coombe. Sat in the sunshine. The distant sheep-bells, the sound of the stream; the woodman winding along the half-marked road with his laden pony;

locks of wool still spangled with the dew-drops; the blue-grey sea shaded with immense masses of cloud, not streaked; the sheep glittering in the sunshine. Returned through the wood. The trees skirting the wood, being exposed more directly to the action of the sea breeze, stripped of the net-work of their upper boughs, which are stiff and erect and like black skeletons; the ground strewed with the red berries of the holly. Set forward before two o'clock. Returned a little after four.

27th. Walked from seven o'clock till half-past eight. Upon the whole an uninteresting evening. Only once while we were in the wood the moon burst through the invisible veil which enveloped her, the shadows of the oaks blackened, and their lines became more strongly marked. The withered leaves were coloured with a deeper yellow, a brighter gloss spotted the hollies; again her form became dimmer; the sky flat, unmarked by distances, a white thin cloud. The manufacturer's dog makes a strange, uncouth howl, which it continues many minutes after there is no noise near it but that of the brook. It howls at the murmur of the village stream.

28th. Walked only to the mill.

29th. A very stormy day. William walked to the top of the hill to see the sea. Nothing distinguishable but a heavy blackness. An immense bough riven from one of the fir trees.

30th. William called me into the garden to observe a singular appearance about the moon. A perfect rainbow, within the bow one star, only of colours more vivid. The semi-circle soon became a complete circle, and in the course of three or four minutes the whole faded away. Walked to the blacksmith's and the baker's; an uninteresting evening.

31st. Set forward to Stowey at half-past five. A violent storm in the wood; sheltered under the hollies. When we left home the moon immensely large, the sky scattered over with clouds. These soon closed in, contracting the dimensions of the moon without concealing her. The sound of the pattering shower, and the gusts of wind, very grand. Left the wood when nothing remained of the storm but the driving wind, and a few scattering drops of rain. Presently all clear, Venus first showing herself between the struggling clouds; afterwards Jupiter appeared. The hawthorn hedges black and pointed, glittering with millions of diamond drops; the hollies shining with broader patches of light. The road to the village of Holford glittered like another stream. On our return, the wind high – a violent storm of hail and rain at the Castle of Comfort. All the heavens seemed in one perpetual motion when the rain ceased; the moon appearing, now half veiled, and now retired behind heavy clouds, the stars still moving, the roads very dirty.

Sarah Murray, *A Companion and Useful Guide to the Beauties of Scotland* (1799)

Another day I walked to the foot of the great lake [Loch Ness], passing by some old monastic ruins, on a small peninsula between the great lake and the branch of it opposite Dochfour house. Few scenes can be found more majestic than that, viewed from the foot of the lake, and under the red cliff mountain on the north side, and even all the way to the entrance into Glen Urquhart. The whole of Loch Ness is before you in front. Its length is twenty-four miles; its breadth, from two to two miles and a half; perfectly straight, running from south-west to northeast; completely filling the space between the sublime over-hanging mountains, with summits in the clouds; some covered with wood, others rearing up, from a bold base, their craggy heads, frowning majestically over the wide glassy vista beneath them, fading in the horizon, while the tops of the distant mountains mellowed down to the softest shades, till all is lost in unison with the clouds, sweeping behind the nearer, and huge projecting sides of Meal-four-vounie, lying between Glen Urquhart and Glen Morrison. The mountain called Meal-four-vounie [Meall Fuar-mhonaidh] is 3,060 feet above the level of the sea; and viewed at a distance, is a prodigiously fine object, towering above its neighbours; but near, it becomes, as its Galic name denotes, a lump of cold moor; though the side of it on Loch Ness is clothed with wood to the water's edge. There is a lake of cold fresh water upon the top of Meal-four-vounie, the depth of which cannot be fathomed. The country people affirm, if any thing be put into the lake at the top of the mountain at night, it is sure to be found in the morning in the great lake below. From the foot of the great lake, I continued the road on the north side, under the grand sweeping mountains of Red hill, &c; nothing but the road, the width of a cart between the hills and the lake, and that often on a shelf cut out of the rocks, hanging over the water; with continued patches of alder, birch, whins, and mountain ash; and ash tress bending over the crags to the lake, and creeping up the rugged mountains' sides. Here and there wide channels filled with round loose stones, brought down from the mountains by torrents and burns, in hard rains. The projecting shore on which the grand ruin of Castle Urquhart stands, forms a noble object in the view; and the bold rocks and woods of the southern bank complete this truly sublime scene. I was unable to walk as far as the beginning of Glen Urquhart; but I was told it is a perfect Eden. The fine ruin of the castle of Urquhart, erected by the Cummings, and demolished by King Edward, now belongs to Sir James Grant. It seems the inhabitants of Glen Urquhart are wedded to it, that not one native has quitted it, nor one foreigner taken up an abode therein, for ninety years. There is also a curious well, of which women drink after childbirth, instead of being churched.

With great regret I turned my back on this grand scene; but my legs would carry me no further, I was therefore obliged to submit.

Dorothy Wordsworth,
The Grasmere Journal (1800)

May 14th, 1800. Wm & John set off into Yorkshire after dinner at ½ past 2 o'clock – cold pork in their pockets. I left them at the turning of the Low-wood bay under the trees. My heart was so full that I could hardly speak to W when I gave him a farewell kiss. I sate a long time upon a stone at the margin of the lake, & after a flood of tears my heart was easier. The lake looked to me, I knew not why, dull and melancholy, the weltering on the shores seemed a heavy sound. I walked as long as I could amongst the stones of the shore. The wood rich in flowers. A beautiful yellow, palish yellow flower, that looked thick round & double, & smelt very sweet – I supposed it was a ranunculus – Crowfoot, the grassy-leaved Rabbit-toothed white flower, strawberries, Geranium – scentless violet, anemones two kinds, orchises, primroses. The heckberry very beautiful as a low shrub. The crab coming out. Met a blind man driving a very large beautiful Bull & a cow – he walked with two sticks. Came home by Clappersgate. The valley very green, many sweet views up to Rydale head when I could juggle away the fine houses, but they disturbed me even more than when I have been happier – one beautiful view of the Bridge, without Sir Michaels. Sate down very often, tho' it was cold.

I resolved to write a journal of the time till W & J return, & I set about keeping my resolve because I will not quarrel with myself, & because I shall give Wm Pleasure by it when he comes home again. At Rydale a woman of the village, stout & well-dressed, begged a halfpenny – she had never she said done it before – but these hard times! – Arrived at home with a bad head-ach, set some slips of privett. The evening cold had a fire – my face now flame-coloured. It is nine o'clock, I shall soon go to bed. A young woman begged at the door – she had come from Manchester on Sunday morn with two shillings & a slip of paper which she supposed a Bank note – it was a cheat. She had buried her husband & three children within a year & a half – All in one grave – burying very dear – paupers all put in one place – 20 shillings paid for as much ground as will bury a man – a grave stone to be put over it or the right will be lost – 11/6 each time the ground is opened. Oh! that I had a letter from William!

May 15, Thursday. A coldish dull morning – hoed the first row of peas, weeded &c &c – sat hard to mending till evening. The rain which had threatened all day came on just when I was going to walk –

Friday morning. Warm & mild after a fine night of rain. Transplanted raddishes after breakfast. Walked to Mr Gells with the Books – gathered mosses & plants. The woods extremely beautiful with all autumnal variety & softness – I carried a basket for mosses, & gathered some wild plants – Oh! that we had a book of botany – all flowers now are gay & deliciously sweet. The primrose still pre-eminent among the later flowers of the spring. Foxgloves very tall – with their heads budding. I went forward round the lake at the foot of Loughrigg fell – I was much amused with the business of a pair of stone chats. Their restless voices as they skimmed along the water following each other their shadows under them, & their returning back to the stones on the shore, chirping with the same unwearied voice. Could not cross the water so I went round by the stepping stones. The morning clear but cloudy, that is the hills were not overhung by mists. After dinner Aggy weeded onions & carrots – I helped for a little – wrote to Mary Hutchinson – washed my head – worked. After tea went to Ambleside – a pleasant cool but not cold evening. Rydale was very beautiful with spear-shaped streaks of polished steel. No letters! – only one newspaper. I returned by Clappersgate. Grasmere was very solemn in the last glimpse of twilight it calls home the heart to quietness. I had been very melancholy in my walk back. I had many of my saddest thoughts & I could not keep the tears within me. But when I came to Grasmere I felt that it did me good. I finished my letter to MH. – ate hasty pudding, & went to bed. As I was going out in the morning I met a half crazy old man. He shewed me a pincushion, & begged a pin, afterwards a halfpenny. He began in a kind of indistinct voice in this manner 'Matthew Jobson's lost a cow. Tom Nichol has two good horses strained – Jim Jones's cow's brokken her horn, &c &c – ' He went into Aggys & persuaded her to give him some whey & let him boil some porridge. She declares he ate two quarts.

Saturday. Incessant rain from morning till night. T. Ashburner brought us coals. Worked hard & Read Midsummer night's dream, Ballads – sauntered a little in the garden. The Skobby sate quietly in its nest rocked by the winds & beaten by the rain.

Sunday, 18th. Went to church, slight showers, a cold air. The mountains from this window look much greener & I think the valley is more green than ever. The corn begins to shew itself. The ashes are still bare. Went part of the way home with Miss Simpson – A little girl from Coniston came to beg. She had lain out all night – her step-mother had turn'd her out of doors. Her father could not stay at home 'She flights so.' Walked to Ambleside in the evening round the lake. The prospect exceeding beautiful from Loughrigg Fell. It was so green, that no eye could be weary of reposing upon it. The most beautiful situation for a house in the field next to Mr Benson's. It threatened rain all evening but was mild & pleasant. I was overtaken by 2 Cumberland people on the other side of Rydale who complimented me upon my walking. They were going to sell cloth, & odd things which they make themselves in Hawkshead & the neighbourhood. The post was not arrived so I walked thro the town, past Mrs Taylors, & met him. Letters from Coleridge & Cottle – John Fisher overtook me on the other side of Rydale – he talked much about the alteration in the times, & observed that in a short time there would be only two ranks of people, the very rich & the very poor, for those who have small estates says he are forced to sell, & all the land goes into one hand. Did not reach home till 10 o clock.

Monday. Sauntered a good deal in the garden, bound carpets, mended old clothes. Read Timon of Athens. Dried linen

– Molly weeded the turnips, John stuck the peas. We had not much sunshine or wind but no rain till about 7 o'clock when we had a slight shower just after I had set out upon my walk. I did not return but walked up into the Black quarter. I sauntered a long time among the rocks above the church. The most delightful situation possible for a cottage commanding two distinct views of the vale & of the lake, is among those rocks – I strolled on, gathered mosses, &c. The quietness & still seclusion of the valley affected me even to producing the deepest melancholy – I forced myself from it. The wind rose before I went to bed. No rain – Dodwell & Wilkinson called in my absence.

Tuesday Morning. A fine mild rain – after Breakfast the sky cleared & before the clouds passed from the hill, I went to Ambleside – It was a sweet morning – Everything green & overflowing with life, & the streams making a perpetual song with the thrushes & all little birds, not forgetting the Stone chats. The post was not come in – I walked as far as Windermere & met him there. No letters! no papers. Came home by Clappersgate – I was sadly tired, ate a hasty dinner & had a bad head-ach, went to bed & slept at least 2 hours. Rain came on in the Evening – Molly washing.

Wednesday. Went often to spread the linen which was bleaching – a rainy day & very wet night.

Thursday A very fine day with showers – dried the linen & starched Drank tea at Mr Simpsons. Brought down Batchelors Buttons (Rock Ranunculus) & other plants – went part of the way back. A showery, mild evening – all the peas up.

Friday, 23rd. Ironing till tea time. So heavy a rain that I could not go for letters – put by the linen, mended stockings &c.

Saturday, May 24th. Walked in the morning to Ambleside. I found a letter from Wm & from Mary Hutchinson & Douglass. Returned on the other side of the lakes – wrote to William after dinner – nailed up the beds worked in the garden – Sate in the evening under the trees. I went to bed soon with a bad head-ach – a fine day.

Sunday. A very fine warm day – had no fire. Read Macbeth in the morning – sate under the trees after dinner. Miss Simpson came just as I was going out & she sate with me. I wrote to my Brother Christopher, & sent John Fisher to Ambleside after tea. Miss Simpson & I walked to the foot of the lake – her Brother met us. I went with them nearly home & on my return found a letter from Coleridge & from Charles Lloyd & three papers.

Monday, May 26. A very fine morning, worked in the garden till after 10 when old Mr Simpson came & talked to me till after 12. Molly weeding. Wrote letters to J H, Coleridge, C Ll. & W. I walked towards Rydale & turned aside at my favorite field. The air & the lake were still – one cottage light in the vale, had so much of day left that I could distinguish objects, the woods; trees & houses. Two or three different kinds of Birds sang at intervals on the opposite shore. I sate till I could hardly drag myself away I grew so sad. 'When pleasant thoughts &c –'

Tuesday, 27th. I walked to Ambleside with letters – met the post before I reached Mr Partridges, one paper, only a letter for Coleridge – I expected a letter from Wm. It was a sweet morning, the ashes in the valleys nearly in full leaf but still to be distinguished, quite bare on the higher grounds. I was warm in returning, & becoming cold with sitting in the house – I had a bad head-ach – went to bed after dinner, & lay till after 5 – not well after tea. I worked in the garden, but did not walk further. A delightful evening before the Sun set but afterwards it grew colder. Mended stockings &c.

Wednesday. In the morning walked up to the rocks above Jenny Dockeray's – sate a long time upon the grass the prospect divinely beautiful. If I had three hundred pounds & could afford to have a bad interest for my money I would buy that estate, & we would build a cottage there to end our days in – I went into her garden & got white & yellow lilies, periwinkle &c, which I planted. Sate under the trees with my work – no fire in the morning. Worked till between 7 & 8, & then watered the garden, & was about to go up to Mr Simpson's, when Miss S & her visitors passed the door. I went home with them, a beautiful evening the crescent moon hanging above helm crag.

Thursday. In the morning worked in the garden a little, read King John. Miss Simpson & Miss Falcon & Mr S came very early – went to Mr Gells boat before tea – we fished upon the lake & amongst us caught 13 Bass. Miss Simpson brought gooseberries & *cream* left the water at near nine o clock, very cold. Went part of the way home with the party.

Friday. In the morning went to Ambleside, forgetting that the post does not come till the evening – how was I grieved when I was so informed – I walked back resolving to go again in the evening. It rained very mildly & sweetly in the morning as I came home, but came on a wet afternoon & evening – luckily I caught Mr Ollifs Lad as he was going for letters, he brought me one from Wm & 12 papers. I planted London pride upon the wall & many things on the Borders. John sodded the wall. As I came past Rydale in the morning I saw a Heron swimming with only its neck out of water – it beat & struggled amongst the water when it flew away & was long in getting loose.

Saturday. A sweet mild rainy morning. Grundy the carpet man called I paid him 1 – 10/ – Went to the Blind man's for plants. I got such a load that I was obliged to leave my Basket in the Road & send Molly for it. Planted &c. After dinner when I was putting up vallances Miss Simpson & her Visitors called – I went with them to Brathay Bridge. We got Broom in returning, strawberries &c, came home by Ambleside – Grasmere looked divinely beautiful. Mr, Miss Simpson & Tommy drank tea at 8 o clock – I walked to the Potters with them.

Sunday, June 1st. Rain in the night – a sweet mild morning – Read Ballads, went to church. Singers from Wytheburn. Went part of the way home with Miss Simpson. Walked upon the hill above the house till dinner-time – went again to church – a Christening & singing which kept us very late. The pew-side came down with me. Walked with Miss Simpson nearly home. After tea went to Ambleside, round the lakes – a very fine warm evening. I lay upon the steep of Loughrigg my heart dissolved in what I saw when I was not startled but recalled from my reverie by a noise as of a child paddling without shoes. I looked up and saw a lamb close to me – it approached nearer & nearer as if to examine me & stood a long time. I did not move – at last it ran past me & went bleating along the pathway seeming to be seeking its mother. I saw a hare in the high road. The post was not come in. I waited in the Road till Johns apprentice came with a letter from Coleridge & 3 papers. The moon shone upon the water – reached home at 10 o clock – went to bed immediately. Molly brought Daisies &c which we planted.

Monday. A cold dry windy morning. I worked in the garden & planted flowers &c – Sate under the trees after dinner till tea time. John Fisher stuck the peas, Molly weeded & washed. I went to Ambleside after tea, crossed the stepping-stones at the foot of Grasmere & pursued my way on the other side of Rydale & by Clappersgate. I sate a long time to watch the hurrying waves & to hear the regularly irregular sound of the dashing waters. The waves round about the little seemed like a dance of spirits that rose out of the water, round its small circumference of shore. Inquired about lodgings for Coleridge, & was accompanied by Mrs Nicholson as far as Rydale. This was very kind, but God be thanked I want not society by a moonlight lake – It was near 11 when I reached home. I wrote to Coleridge & went late to bed.

Tuesday. Sent off my letter by the Butcher – a boisterous drying day. Worked in the garden before dinner. Read Rd Second

– was not well after dinner & lay down. Mrs Simpsons grand-
son brought me some gooseberries – I got up & walked with
him part of the way home, afterwards went rambling by the
lake side – got Lockety goldings, strawberries &c, & planted.
After tea the wind fell I walked towards Mr Simpsons. Gave
the newspapers to the Girl, reached home at 10. No letter, no
William – a letter from Rd to John.

Wednesday. A very fine day. I sate out of doors most of the day,
wrote to Mr Jackson. Ambleside fair. I walked to the lake side
in the morning, took up plants & sate upon a stone reading
Ballads. In the Evening I was watering plants when Mr & Miss
Simpson called – I accompanied them home – & we went to
the waterfall at the head of the valley – it was very interesting
in the Twilight. I brought home lemon thyme & several other
plants, & planted them by moonlight. I lingered out of doors
in the hope of hearing my Brothers tread.

Thursday. I sate out of doors great part of the day & worked in
the Garden – had a letter from Mr Jackson, & wrote an answer
to Coleridge. The little birds busy making love & pecking the
blossoms & bits of moss off the trees, they flutter about &
about & thrid the trees as I lie under them. Molly went out to
tea – I would not go far from home expecting my Brothers –
I rambled on the hill above the house gathered wild thyme &
took up roots of wild Columbine. Just as I was returning with
my 'load', Mr & Miss Simpson called. We went again upon
the hill, got more plants, set them, & then went to the Blind
Mans for London Pride for Miss Simpson. I went up with
them as far as the Blacksmith's. A fine lovely moonlight night.

Friday. Sate out of doors reading the Whole Afternoon, but in the morning I wrote to my aunt Cookson. In the Evening I went to Ambleside with Coleridge's letter – it was a lovely night as the day had been. I went by Loughrigg & Clappersgate & just met the post at the turnpike – he told me there were two letters but none for me. So I was in no hurry & went round again by Clappersgate, crossed the Stepping stones & entered Ambleside at Matthew Harrisons – A letter from Jack Hutchinson, & one from Montagu enclosing a 3£ note – No William! I slackened my pace as I came near home fearing to hear that he was not come. I listened till after one o'clock to every barking dog, Cock fighting, & other sports: it was Mr Borricks opening. Foxgloves just coming into blossom.

Saturday. A very warm cloudy morning, threatening to rain. I walked up to Mr Simpsons to gather gooseberries – it was a very fine afternoon – little Tommy came down with me, ate gooseberry pudding & drank tea with me. We went up the hill to gather sods & plants & went down to the lake side & took up orchises &c – I watered the garden & weeded. I did not leave home in the expectation of Wm & John, & sitting at work till after 11 o clock I heard a foot go to the front of the house, turn round, & open the gate. It was William – after our first joy was over we got some tea. We did not go to bed till 4 o clock in the morning so he had an opportunity of seeing our improvements – the birds were singing, & all looked fresh though not gay. There was a greyness on earth & sky. We did not rise till near 10 in the morning. We were busy all day in writing letters to Coleridge, Montagu, Douglass, Richard. Mr & Miss Simpson called in the Evening, the little Boy carried our letters to Ambleside. We walked with Mr & Miss S home on their return the evening was cold & I was afraid of the tooth-ach for William. We met John on our return home.

Jane Austen to Cassandra Austen,
May 1801

21–22 May 1801

Our grand walk to Weston was again fixed for Yesterday, & was accomplished in a very striking manner; Everyone of the party declined it under some pretence or other except our two selves [a Mrs Chamberlayne and Jane Austen], & we had therefore a tete á tete; but *that* we should equally have had after the first two Yards, had half the inhabitants of Bath set off with us. – It would have amused you to see our progress; – we went up by Sion Hill, & returned across the fields; – in climbing a hill Mrs Chamberlayne is very capital; I could with difficulty keep pace with her – yet would not flinch for the World. – on plain ground I was quite her equal – and so we posted away under a fine hot sun, *She* without any parasol or shade to her hat, stopping for nothing, & crossing the Church Yard at Weston with as much expedition as if we were afraid of being buried alive. – After seeing what she is equal to, I cannot help feeling a regard for her.

26–27 May 1801

My adventures since I wrote to you three days ago have been such as the time would easily contain; I walked yesterday morning with Mrs Chamberlayne to Lyncombe & Widcombe, and in the evening I drank tea with the Holders. – Mrs Chamberlayne's pace was not quite so magnificent on this second trial as in the first; it was nothing more than I could keep up with, without effort; & for many, many Yards together on a raised narrow footpath I led the way. – The Walk was very beautiful as my companion agreed, whenever I made the observation – And so ends our freindship [*sic*], for the Chamberlaynes leave Bath in a day or two.

Jane Austen, *Pride and Prejudice* (1813)

'Well, my dear,' said Mr Bennet, when Elizabeth had read the note aloud, 'if your daughter should have a dangerous fit of illness, if she should die, it would be a comfort to know that it was all in pursuit of Mr Bingley, and under your orders.'

'Oh! I am not at all afraid of her dying. People do not die of little trifling colds. She will be taken good care of. As long as she stays there, it is all very well. I would go and see her, if I could have the carriage.'

Elizabeth, feeling really anxious, was determined to go to her, though the carriage was not to be had; and as she was no horsewoman, walking was her only alternative. She declared her resolution.

'How can you be so silly,' cried her mother, 'as to think of such a thing, in all this dirt! You will not be fit to be seen when you get there.'

'I shall be very fit to see Jane – which is all I want.'

'Is this a hint to me, Lizzy,' said her father, 'to send for the horses?'

'No, indeed. I do not wish to avoid the walk. The distance is nothing, when one has a motive; only three miles. I shall be back by dinner.'

'I admire the activity of your benevolence,' observed Mary, 'but every impulse of feeling should be guided by reason; and, in my opinion, exertion should always be in proportion to what is required.'

'We will go as far as Meryton with you,' said Catherine and Lydia. Elizabeth accepted their company, and the three young ladies set off together.

'If we make haste,' said Lydia, as they walked along, 'perhaps we may see something of Captain Carter before he goes.'

In Meryton they parted: the two youngest repaired to the lodgings of one of the officers' wives, and Elizabeth continued her walk alone, crossing field after field at a pace, jumping over stiles and springing over puddles with impatient activity, and finding herself at last within view of the house, with weary ankles, dirty stockings, and a face glowing with the warmth of exercise.

She was shown into the breakfast-parlour, where all but Jane were assembled, and where her appearance created a great deal of surprise. That she should have walked three miles so early in the day, in such dirty weather, and by herself, was almost incredible to Mrs. Hurst and Miss Bingley; and Elizabeth was convinced that they held her in contempt for it. She was received, however, very politely by them; and in their brother's manners there was something better than politeness; there was good humour and kindness.

Mary Shelley, *History of a Six Weeks' Tour through a Part of France, Switzerland, Germany and Holland* (1817)

After remaining a week in Paris, we received a small remittance that set us free from a kind of imprisonment there which we found very irksome. But how should we proceed? After talking over and rejecting many plans, we fixed on one eccentric enough, but which, from its romance, was very pleasing to us. In England we could not have put it in execution without sustaining continual insult and impertinence: the French are far more tolerant of the vagaries of their neighbours. We resolved to walk through France; but as I was too weak for any considerable distance, and my sister could not be supposed to be able to walk as far as S*** each day, we determined to purchase an ass, to carry our portmanteau and one of us by turns.

Early, therefore, on Monday, August 8th, S*** and C*** went to the ass market, and purchased an ass, and the rest of the day, until four in the afternoon, was spent in preparations for our departure; during which, Madam L'Hôte paid us a visit, and attempted to dissuade us from our design. She represented to us that a large army had been recently disbanded, that the soldiers and officers wandered idle about the country, and that *les Dames seroient certainement enlevèes*. But we were proof against her arguments, and packing up a few necessaries, leaving the rest to go by the diligence, we departed in a fiacre from the door of the hotel, our little ass following.

We dismissed the coach at the barrier. It was dusk and the ass seemed totally unable to bear one of us, appearing to sink under the portmanteau, although it was small and light. We were, however, merry enough, and thought the leagues short. We arrived at Charenton about ten.

Charenton is prettily situated in a valley, through which the Seine flows, winding among banks variegated with trees. On looking at this scene, C*** exclaimed, 'Oh! this is beautiful enough; let us live here.' This was her exclamation on every new scene, and as each surpassed the one before, she cried, 'I am glad we did not stay at Charenton, but let us live here.'

Finding our ass useless, we sold it before we proceeded on our journey and bought a mule, for ten Napoleons. About nine o'clock we departed. We were clad in black silk. I rode on the mule, which carried also our portmanteau; S*** and C*** followed, bringing a small basket of provisions. At about one we arrived at Gros Bois, where, under the shade of trees, we ate our bread and fruit, and drank our wine, thinking of Don Quixote and Sancho.

The country through which we passed was highly cultivated, but uninteresting; the horizon scarcely ever extended beyond the circumference of a few fields, bright and waving with the golden harvest. We met several travellers; but our mode, although novel, did not appear to excite any curiosity or remark.

Jane Austen, *Persuasion* (1818)

It was a very fine November day, and the Miss Musgroves came through the little grounds, and stopped for no other purpose than to say, that they were going to take a *long* walk, and, therefore, concluded Mary could not like to go with them; and when Mary immediately replied, with some jealousy, at not being supposed a good walker, 'Oh, yes, I should like to join you very much, I am very fond of a long walk,' Anne felt persuaded, by the looks of the two girls, that it was precisely what they did not wish, and admired again the sort of necessity which the family-habits seemed to produce, of every thing being to be communicated, and every thing being to be done together, however undesired and inconvenient. She tried to dissuade Mary from going, but in vain; and that being the case, thought it best to accept the Miss Musgroves' much more cordial invitation to herself to go likewise, as she might be useful in turning back with her sister, and lessening the interference in any plan of their own.

'I cannot imagine why they should suppose I should not like a long walk!' said Mary, as she went up stairs. 'Every body is always supposing that I am not a good walker! And yet they would not have been pleased, if we had refused to join them.

When people come in this manner on purpose to ask us, how can one say no?'

Just as they were setting off, the gentlemen returned. They had taken out a young dog, who had spoilt their sport, and sent them back early. Their time and strength, and spirits, were, therefore, exactly ready for this walk, and they entered into it with pleasure. Could Anne have foreseen such a junction, she would have staid at home; but, from some feelings of interest and curiosity, she fancied now that it was too late to retract, and the whole six set forward together in the direction chosen by the Miss Musgroves, who evidently considered the walk as under their guidance.

Anne's object was, not to be in the way of any body; and where the narrow paths across the fields made many separations necessary, to keep with her brother and sister. Her *pleasure* in the walk must arise from the exercise and the day, from the view of the last smiles of the year upon the tawny leaves, and withered hedges, and from repeating to herself some few of the thousand poetical descriptions extant of autumn, that season of peculiar and inexhaustible influence on the mind of taste and tenderness, that season which has drawn from every poet, worthy of being read, some attempt at description, or some lines of feeling.

Mary Shelley, *Frankenstein; or, The Modern Prometheus* (1818)

My first resolution was to quit Geneva for ever; my country, which, when I was happy and beloved, was dear to me, now, in my adversity, became hateful. I provided myself with a sum of money, together with a few jewels which had belonged to my mother, and departed.

And now my wanderings began, which are to cease but with life. I have traversed a vast portion of the earth, and have endured all the hardships which travellers, in deserts and barbarous countries, are wont to meet. How I have lived I hardly know; many times have I stretched my failing limbs upon the sandy plain, and prayed for death. But revenge kept me alive; I dared not die, and leave my adversary in being.

When I quitted Geneva, my first labour was to gain some clue by which I might trace the steps of my fiendish enemy. But my plan was unsettled; and I wandered many hours around the confines of the town, uncertain what path I should pursue. As night approached, I found myself at the entrance of the cemetery where William, Elizabeth, and my father, reposed. I entered it, and approached the tomb which marked their graves. Every thing was silent, except the leaves of the trees, which were greatly agitated by the wind; the night was nearly dark; and the scene would have been solemn and affecting even to an uninterested observer. The spirits of the departed seemed to flit around, and to cast a shadow, which was felt but not seen, around the head of the mourner.

The deep grief which this scene had first excited quickly gave way to rage and despair. They were dead, and I lived; their murderer also lived, and to destroy him I must drag out my weary existence. I knelt on the grass, and kissed the earth, and with quivering lips exclaimed, 'By the sacred earth on which I kneel, by the shades that wander near me, by the deep and eternal grief that I feel, I swear; and by thee, O Night, and by the spirits that preside over thee, I swear to pursue the dæmon, who caused this misery, until he or I shall perish in mortal conflict. For this purpose I will preserve my life: to execute this dear revenge, will I again behold the sun, and tread the green herbage of earth, which otherwise should vanish from my eyes for ever. And I call on you, spirits of the dead; and on you, wandering ministers of vengeance, to aid and conduct me in my work. Let the cursed and hellish monster drink deep of agony; let him feel the despair that now torments me.'

I had begun my adjurations with solemnity, and an awe which almost assured me that the shades of my murdered friends heard and approved my devotion; but the furies possessed me as I concluded, and rage choked my utterance.

I was answered through the stillness of night by a loud and fiendish laugh. It rung on my ears long and heavily; the mountains re-echoed it, and I felt as if all hell surrounded me with mockery and laughter. Surely in that moment I should have been possessed by phrenzy, and have destroyed my miserable existence, but that my vow was heard, and that

I was reserved for vengeance. The laughter died away; when a well-known and abhorred voice, apparently close to my ear, addressed me in an audible whisper – 'I am satisfied: miserable wretch! you have determined to live, and I am satisfied.'

I darted towards the spot from which the sound proceeded; but the devil eluded my grasp. Suddenly the broad disk of the moon arose, and shone full upon his ghastly and distorted shape, as he fled with more than mortal speed.

I pursued him; and for many months this has been my task. Guided by a slight clue, I followed the windings of the Rhone, but vainly. The blue Mediterranean appeared; and, by a strange chance, I saw the fiend enter by night, and hide himself in a vessel bound for the Black Sea. I took my passage in the same ship; but he escaped, I know not how.

Amidst the wilds of Tartary and Russia, although he still evaded me, I have ever followed his track. Sometimes the peasants, scared by this horrid apparition, informed me of his path; sometimes he himself, who feared that if I lost all trace I should despair and die, often left some mark to guide me. The snows descended on my head, and I saw the print of his huge step on the white plain. To you first entering on life, to whom care is new, and agony unknown, how can you understand what I have felt, and still feel? Cold, want, and fatigue, were the least pains which I was destined to endure; I was cursed by some devil, and carried about with me my eternal hell; yet still a spirit of good followed and directed my steps, and, when I most murmured, would suddenly extricate me from seemingly insurmountable difficulties. Sometimes, when nature, overcome by hunger, sunk under the exhaustion, a repast was prepared for me in the desert, that restored and inspirited me. The fare was indeed coarse, such as the peasants of the country ate; but I may not doubt that it was set there by the spirits that I had invoked to aid me. Often, when all was dry, the heavens cloudless, and I was parched by thirst, a slight cloud would bedim the sky, shed a few drops that revived me, and vanish.

I followed, when I could, the courses of the rivers; but the dæmon generally avoided these, as it was here that the population of the country chiefly collected. In other places human beings were seldom seen; and I generally subsisted on the wild animals that crossed my path. I had money with me, and gained the friendship of the villagers by distributing it, or bringing with me some food that I had killed, which, after taking a small part, I always presented to those who had provided me with fire and utensils for cooking.

My life, as it passed thus, was indeed hateful to me, and it was during sleep alone that I could taste joy. O blessed sleep! often, when most miserable, I sank to repose, and my dreams lulled me even to rapture. The spirits that guarded me had provided these moments, or rather hours, of happiness, that I might retain strength to fulfil my pilgrimage. Deprived of this respite, I should have sunk under my hardships. During the day I was sustained and inspirited by the hope of night: for in sleep I saw my friends, my wife, and my beloved country; again I saw the benevolent countenance of my father, heard the silver tones of my Elizabeth's voice, and beheld Clerval enjoying health and youth. Often, when wearied by a toilsome march, I persuaded myself that I was dreaming until night should come, and that I should then enjoy reality in the arms of my dearest friends. What agonizing fondness did I feel for them! how did I cling to their dear forms, as sometimes they haunted even my waking hours, and persuade myself that they still lived! At such moments vengeance, that burned within me, died in my heart, and I pursued my path towards the destruction of the dæmon, more as a task enjoined by heaven, as the mechanical impulse of some power of which I was unconscious, than as the ardent desire of my soul.

What his feelings were whom I pursued, I cannot know. Sometimes, indeed, he left marks in writing on the bark of the trees, or cut in stone, that guided me, and instigated my fury. 'My reign is not yet over,' (these words were legible in one of these inscriptions); 'you live, and my power is complete. Follow me; I seek the everlasting ices of the north, where you will feel the misery of cold and frost, to which I am impassive. You will find near this place, if you follow not too tardily, a dead hare; eat, and be refreshed. Come on, my enemy; we have yet to wrestle for our lives; but many hard and miserable hours must you endure, until that period shall arrive.'

Scoffing devil! Again do I vow vengeance; again do I devote thee, miserable fiend, to torture and death. Never will I omit my search, until he or I perish; and then with what ecstacy shall I join my Elizabeth, and those who even now prepare for me the reward of my tedious toil and pilgrimage.

Dorothy Wordsworth to William Johnson, 21 October 1818

We found ourselves at the top of Ash Course without a weary limb, having had the fresh air of autumn to help us up by its invigorating power, and the sweet warmth of the unclouded sun to tempt us to sit and rest by the way. From the top of Ash Course we beheld a prospect which would indeed have amply repaid us for a *toilsome* journey, if such it had been; and a sense of thankfulness for the continuance of the vigour of body, which enabled me to climb the high mountain, as in the days of my youth, inspiring me with fresh chearfulness, added a delight, a charm to the contemplation of the magnificent scenes before me, which I cannot describe. Still less can I tell you the glories of what we saw. Three views, each distinct in its kind, we saw at once – the vale of Borrowdale, of Keswick, of Bassenthwaite – Skiddaw, Saddleback, Helvellyn, numerous other mountains, and, still beyond, the Solway Firth, and the mountains of Scotland.

Nearer to us, on the other side, and below us, were the Langdale Pikes, then our own Vale below them, Windermere, and far beyond Windermere, after a long distance, Ingleborough in Yorkshire. But how shall I speak of the peculiar deliciousness of the third prospect? At this time *that* was most favoured by sunshine and shade. The green Vale of Esk – deep and green, with its glittering serpent stream was below us; and on we looked to the mountains near the sea – Black Combe and others – and still beyond, to the sea itself in dazzling brightness. Turning round we saw the mountains of Wasdale in tumult; and Great Gavel, though the middle of the mountain was to us as its base, looked very grand.

We had attained the object of our journey; but our ambition mounted higher. We saw the summit of Scaw Fell, as it seemed, very near to us; we were indeed, three parts up that mountain, and thither we determined to go. We found the distance greater than it had appeared to us, but our courage did not fail; however, when we came nearer we perceived that in order to attain that summit we must make a great dip, and that the ascent afterwards would be exceedingly steep and difficult, so that we might have been benighted if we had attempted it; therefore, unwillingly, we gave it up, and resolved, instead, to ascend another point of the same mountain, called *the Pikes*, and which, I have since found, the measurers of the mountains estimate as higher than the larger summit which bears the name of Scaw Fell, and where the Stone Man is built which we, at the time, considered as the point of highest honour. The sun had never once been overshadowed by a cloud during the whole of our progress from the centre of Borrowdale; at the summit of the Pike there was not a breath of air to stir even the papers which we spread out containing our food. There we ate our dinner in summer warmth; and the stillness seemed to be not of this world. We paused, and kept silence to listen, and not a sound of any kind was to be heard. We were far above the reach of the cataracts of Scaw Fell; and not an insect was there to hum in the air. The Vales before described lay in view, and side by side with Eskdale, we now saw the sister Vale of Donnerdale terminated by the Duddon Sands. But the majesty of the mountains below and close to us, is not to be conceived. We now beheld the whole mass of Great Gavel from its base, the Den of Wasdale at our feet, the gulph immeasurable, Grasmere and the other mountains of Crummock, Ennerdale and *its* mountains, and the sea beyond.

While we were looking round after dinner our Guide said that we must not linger long, for we should have a storm. We looked in vain to espy traces of it; for mountains, vales, and the sea were all touched with the clear light of the sun. 'It is there', he said, pointing to the sea beyond Whitehaven, and, sure enough, we there perceived a light cloud, or mist, unnoticeable but by a shepherd, accustomed to watch all mountain bodings. We gazed around again and yet again, fearful to lose the remembrance of what lay before us in that lofty solitude; and then prepared to depart. Meanwhile the air changed to cold, and we saw the tiny vapour swelled into mighty masses of cloud which came boiling over the mountains. Great Gavel, Helvellyn, and Skiddaw were wrapped in storm; yet Langdale and the mountains in that quarter were all bright with sunshine. Soon the storm reached us; we sheltered under a crag, and almost as rapidly as it had come, it passed away, and left us free to observe the goings-on of storm and sunshine in other quarters – Langdale had now its share, and the Pikes were decorated by two splendid rainbows; Skiddaw also had its own rainbows, but we were glad to see them and the clouds disappear from that mountain, as we knew that Mr. and Mrs. Wilberforce and the family (if they kept the intention which they had formed when they parted from us the night before) must certainly be upon Skiddaw at that very time – and so it was. They were there, and had much more rain than we had; we, indeed, were hardly at all wetted; and before we found ourselves again upon that part of the mountain called Ash Course every cloud had vanished from every summit.

Do not think we here gave up our spirit of enterprise. No! I had heard much of the grandeur of the view of Wasdale from Stye Head, the point from which Wasdale is first seen in coming by the road from Borrowdale; but though I had been in Wasdale I had never entered the dale by that road, and had often lamented that I had not seen what was so much talked of by travellers. Down to that Pass (for we were yet far above it) we bent our course by the side of Ruddle Gill, a very deep red chasm in the mountains which begins at a spring – that spring forms a stream, which must, at times, be a mighty torrent, as is evident from the channel which it has wrought out – thence by Sprinkling Tarn to Stye Head; and there we sate and looked down into Wasdale. We were now upon Great Gavel which rose high above us. Opposite was Scaw Fell and we heard the roaring of the stream from one of the ravines of that mountain, which, though the bending of Wasdale Head lay between us and Scaw Fell, we could look into, as it were, and the depth of the ravine appeared tremendous; it was black and the crags were awful.

We now proceeded homewards by Stye head Tarn along the road into Borrowdale. Before we reached Stonethwaite a few stars had appeared, and we travelled home in our cart by moonlight.

I ought to have described the last part of our ascent to Scaw Fell Pike. There, not a blade of grass was to be seen – hardly a cushion of moss, and that was parched and brown; and only growing rarely between the huge blocks and stones which cover the summit and lie in heaps all round to a great distance, like skeletons or bones of the earth not wanted at the creation, and there left to be covered with never-dying lichens, which the clouds and dews nourish; and adorn with colours of the most vivid and exquisite beauty, and endless in variety. No gems or flowers can surpass in colouring the beauty of some of these masses of stone which no human eye beholds except the shepherd led thither by chance or traveller by curiosity; and how seldom must this happen!

Sarah Stoddart Hazlitt, *The Journal of Sarah Stoddart Hazlitt*, 16 May 1822

Having gone round all the different and beautiful windings of the Loch I relanded at the same spot from which I embarked, and walked along its banks to Ben Lomond, casting many a lingering look behind as I quitted scenes of such sublime magnificence. The road proceeded by the side of some inferior Lochs, and terraced woods, very stony and rough, till you arrive at the mountain, 3,262 feet in height. and in crossing the most dreary, swampy and pathless part of it, a heavy storm came on, there was not the least shelter, and the heat in climbing such an ascent, together, with the fear of losing myself in such a lonely place almost overcame me, but I guided myself by the direction of the Loch as well as I could, and at last, to my great joy, regained a track, but the road now was stony and difficult, over a wide and dreary moor, full of bogs, till you arrive at Inversnaid Garrison, as it is still called, but it is in fact, merely some ruins of what once was such, in the midst of the Moore. the inhabitable part of which is occupied by a few poor people, and it was by the mere chance of going to beg a drink of water, that I found this bore the name of the Garrison, upon enquiring how far it was to it. They directed me to the ferry over Loch Lomond, after crossing which, I had a most delightful walk on its banks: it is like a carriage road through a gentleman's park, with a hanging wood on your right; the Loch at your feet on the left, backed by Ben Lomon and other mountains. The scenery of this, is a perfect contrast to that of Loch Katrine: here, everything is mild, soothing and delicious to the feelings: you are lulled into a dream of happy sensations, and feel 'disencumbered of this mortal coil.' at least such it was with me. About three or four miles on the road is Tarbut, a beautiful little village with a good Inn, all neatly white washed and looking the picture of cleanliness and comfort – from thence, the road still continues on by the side of the Loch to Luss, a small town at about eight miles distance; every now and then, you pass a few scattered houses and cottages on the banks. At Luss then, I arrived about ten o'clock at night, quite enraptured with my walk, and the great variety of uncommonly beautiful scenery I had passed through in the course of the day.

Ellen Weeton, *Miss Weeton's Journal of a Governess* (1825)

June 15. [1825] At Pont A. I left the mail; it was between 11 and 12 o'clock, for we had stopped above half an hour at Beddgelert, to rest the horse, who, poor thing, had to accomplish the whole journey. During this pausing time, I sat under the shade of a tree in the Inn yard, quite at my ease. At P. A. I sat on the battlement of the Bridge, eating part of the bread and butter which I had brought from home, and then walked slowly to a spot I had noticed in passing, near Llyn Cawellyn, where I had to begin my ascent; and, feeling able and eager, I ventured.

I had got up about one third of the way, when, being thirsty, and a tempting rill just by, I took off my bonnet and bent my head to the water, drinking very comfortably. I had provision in a small bag, but a drinking vessel I had forgotten; the drink – the best of all liquids, I knew the Provider would furnish. It was now near 2 o'clock, as I judged by my shadow; for my watch I had left at home for fear of accidents. Just as I raised my head from the water, I saw a gentleman descending with his guide, at a short distance. They espied me. I had already left the regular path a little, merely to quench my thirst; and now deviated a little more, purposely that they might not distinguish my dress or features, lest, seeing me at any other time, they should know where they had seen me; and I should dread the being pointed at in the road or the street as – 'That is the lady I saw ascending Snowdon, alone!'

The guide, seeing I was out of the path (only because he was in it, if he had but known), called out to me, but I was *quite* deaf. He continued shouting, and I was *forced* to hear; he was telling me to keep to the copper path, &c. I knew the way perfectly well, for my Map and my Guide had been well studied at home. I could find from what the gentleman said, that he imagined I had called for the guide at his dwelling, and finding him engaged upon the mountain, had gone so far to meet him; for he intreated the man to leave him. 'I can do perfectly well now,' he repeatedly said. I never turned my face towards them, but walked as fast as I could, hanging down my head; the Guide again giving me some directions – with the best intentions, I am sure, and partly, I think, as a little stratagem to draw me nearer; but I had no fancy to be the heroine of a tale for him to amuse future employers with, and to describe me as young or old, handsome or plain, ladylike or otherwise; and if he could have drawn me near enough so as to have known me again, next thing, perhaps, I should have figured in some newspaper; or some tourists, glad to fill a page of their journal, would have crammed me there, as 'A singular female!' – I am not thus ambitious. No! No!

To the Guide's civility, I twice called out, 'Thank you!' But now my deafness had left me, I had got a stiff neck. When I had mounted a considerable height above them, I turned, and saw the gentleman standing looking up after me, with his hands on his sides as if in astonishment, and the Guide trudging downwards, vexed perhaps that it should be seen that any body could ascent without him, – and a woman, too! and alone! for the lift of his shoulders seemed to indicate as much.

It was my wish to ascend on the Bettws side, to cross over the summit if practicable, and descend at Llanberris. I knew it would lengthen the journey greatly not to descend where I had commenced, but I did not like to do it. I wished to have an entire range and view down every side. I persevered, and reached the first height; I was now higher than ever I had been in the world before. I had often turned and sat down to rest and look at the prospect, but here I remained some time. I could count at one time, from 10 to 14 lakes, some of them mere pools certainly, and a sea of mountains rising in every direction, like wave beyond wave; not a cloud was to be seen, but a slight haze partly obscured the distance; nearer objects were quite distinct. Had I ascended 1 or 2 days sooner, I should have had a brilliantly clear atmosphere, but timidity had prevented my bringing my resolution to the sticking place sooner. Even this morning, on rising, I felt irresolute. I had passed most of the night disturbed by distressing dreams (and dreams of any kind are very unusual to me), occasioned, I dare say, by the feeling of anxiety with which I had retired to rest; yet I knew that as I was not obliged to go, I could any moment return if I saw a prospect of danger. Here I stood, perched on the ridge like a crow on the point of a pinnacle; not a human creature could I see anywhere; for aught I knew, I had the whole mountain to myself.

Dorothy Wordsworth, 'Thoughts on My Sick-Bed' (1832)

And has the remnant of my life
Been pilfered of this sunny Spring?
And have its own prelusive sounds
Touched in my heart no echoing string?

Ah! say not so – the hidden life
Couchant within this feeble frame
Hath been enriched by kindred gifts,
That, undesired, unsought-for, came

With joyful heart in youthful days
When fresh each season in its Round
I welcomed the earliest Celandine
Glittering upon the mossy ground;

With busy eyes I pierced the lane
In quest of known and unknown things,
– The primrose a lamp on its fortress rock,
The silent butterfly spreading its wings,

The violet betrayed by its noiseless breath,
The daffodil dancing in the breeze,
The caroling thrush, on his naked perch,
Towering above the budding trees.

Our cottage-hearth no longer our home,
Companions of Nature were we,
The Stirring, the Still, the Loquacious, the Mute –
To all we gave our sympathy.

Yet never in those careless days
When spring-time in rock, field, or bower
Was but a fountain of earthly hope
A promise of fruits & the splendid flower.

No! then I never felt a bliss
That might with that compare
Which, piercing to my couch of rest,
Came on the vernal air.

When loving Friends an offering brought,
The first flowers of the year,
Culled from the precincts of our home,
From nooks to Memory dear.

With some sad thoughts the work was done.
Unprompted and unbidden,
But joy it brought to my hidden life,
To consciousness no longer hidden.

I felt a power unfelt before,
Controlling weakness, languor, pain;
It bore me to the Terrace walk
I trod the Hills again; –

No prisoner in this lonely room,
I saw the green Banks of the Wye,
Recalling thy prophetic words,
Bard, Brother, Friend from infancy!

No need of motion, or of strength,
Or even the breathing air;
– I thought of Nature's loveliest scenes;
And with Memory I was there.

Charlotte Brontë to Emily Jane Brontë, 2 September 1843

Dear E. J.,

Another opportunity of writing to you coming to pass, I shall improve it by scribbling a few lines. More than half the holidays are now past, and rather better than I expected. The weather has been exceedingly fine during the last fortnight, and yet not so Asiatically hot as it was last year at this time. Consequently I have tramped about a great deal and tried to get a clearer acquaintance with the streets of Bruxelles. This week, as no teacher is here except Mdlle. Blanche, who is returned from Paris, I am always alone except at meal-times, for Mdlle. Blanche's character is so false and so contemptible I can't force myself to associate with her. She perceives my utter dislike and never now speaks to me – a great relief.

However, I should inevitably fall into the gulf of low spirits if I stayed always by myself here without a human being to speak to, so I go out and traverse the Boulevards and streets of Bruxelles sometimes for hours together. Yesterday I went on a pilgrimage to the cemetery, and far beyond it on to a hill where there was nothing but fields as far as the horizon. When I came back it was evening; but I had such a repugnance to return to the house, which contained nothing that I cared for, I still kept threading the streets in the neighbourhood of the Rue d'Isabelle and avoiding it. I found myself opposite to Ste. Gudule, and the bell, whose voice you know, began to toll for evening salut. I went in, quite alone (which procedure you will say is not much like me), wandered about the aisles where a few old women were saying their prayers, till vespers begun. I stayed till they were over.

Harriet Martineau, *A Year at Ambleside* (1845)

January

After a long illness, during which I never saw a tree in leaf for upwards of five years, and passed my life between bed and my sofa, I recovered – to my own surprise, and that of everyone who knew me. In September, I crept out of doors, and lay on a bit of grass a few yards square. In October, I walked down to the seashore, and by degrees extended my rambles to a fine beach three miles from home. By this time there was no doubt of my being well; but it was evidently desirable to change the scene, and break off all associations of sickness with my daily habits, and I eagerly accepted the invitation of friends who lived on the banks of Windermere, to spend a month with them. That month determined my place of residence for, probably, the rest of my life.

I had seen the Lake district in a cursory way, some years before, merely passing through it on my way to Scotland. Its beauty had struck me with a kind of amazement. As I looked down into some of the vales, or around upon a wall of mountains, I was almost incredulous of what I saw. If I had been told that after a long and dreary season of hopeless illness, I should come and sit down for life in this region, I should have looked upon the prospect as one of the most marvellous of the shifting scenes of life. Its beauty is not the only, nor to some people, the chief interest and charm of the Lake district. The mountains, by their conservative influence, have here hedged in a piece of old English life, such as is to be found nowhere else within the island. They have always hedged in a piece of the life that had passed away from the rest of the country. When the Romans were elsewhere building walls around the towns, and stretching out roads from point to point of the island, the Druids were still collecting their assemblage of wild Britons under the foresty shades of this region. The remains of coppices of oak, ash, birch and hollies, show how high up the mountain sides the ancient forest extended and under those trees stood of old the long-bearded, shaven-headed, white robed Druidical priests, sending up a flame of sacrifices, which scared the red deer, and the wolf, and the wild bull in their coverts, and brought the eagles from their highest perch by the scent of prey. But even here changes must come, though later than elsewhere, and the Romans drew near, at last, to invade the region, and pave a road through it. It must have been a curious sight to the skin-clad Britons who were posted as sentinels, when the Roman standards appeared among the trees, and helmets and spears glittered in the pathways of the woods. The Romans took possession of Windermere, and made a camp at its head. If the circles of stones planted by the Druids are visible here and there in the district, no less distinct are the marks of Roman occupation. In a field at the head of Windermere, the outlines of their camp are obvious enough to the eye; and on a mountain ridge, still called High Street, are the fragments of pavement, which show that even here, above the highest tree-tops from which the British sentinels could look forth, the Roman soldiers made a road for their standards and their troops. What a sight it must have been from below. How the native mother must have shrunk back with her children into the caves of the rock, or the covert of the wood – less afraid of the wild beasts than of these majestic invaders, against whom her husband was gone out with his scythe or his club! How she and her companions must have listened to the shock of falling trees, and the cleaving of the rocks, which gave notice that the enemy were making themselves a broad highway through the heart of the district. I always think of those cowering Britons now, when I go by the old Roman road, which descends upon Grasmere. The scene is open enough now, but I can conjure up the forests which clothed the mountain slopes down to the very brink of the Grasmere lake, in the days when the wild boar came down to drink, and the squirrel could (as the country people tell) go from Wythburn to Keswick – ten miles on a straight line – on the tree-tops, without touching the ground.

After all, the Romans passed away before the Britons. The natives remained in considerable numbers in the fastnesses, when the glittering soldiers were no more seen on the paved ways, and the trumpets no longer echoed from one mountain peak to another. But the Saxons and Danes came in to take possession of the fertile spots as the Romans left them. They never obtained possession of the district, however. For six hundred years, the Saxons held some of the fine alluvial lands about the lakes, and lived in settlements where there were natural facilities, for defence; but they needed all these facilities, for the Britons had learned from the Romans how to arm themselves better, and to fight; and for those six hundred years they held their ravines, and forests, and even their villages and hamlets, so that the Saxons could never feel secure. After those six centuries, more and more Saxons crowded to these West Moorlands, now called Westmoreland; but they came not to conquer territory, but to seek shelter from the Normans, who were upon their heels. The Saxon men of substance, who were driven out from their estates in the south by the Norman invaders – robbed, oppressed, outraged in every way – came up among the Fells to nourish vengeance, and form themselves into bands of outlaws, for the torment of as many Roman usurpers as they could reach. The Britons had long ceased to appear elsewhere; and from this time we hear no more of them among the Fells, and, as before, the Saxons were to be heard of as holding the Fells, long after their race had mingled with the Normans everywhere to the south. The Normans came as near as they could, but they never so far penetrated the West Moorlands as to build castles in the midst, and settle down there as inhabitants. They obtained grants of land, but they never practically took possession of them. They built monasteries and castles in the level country which stretches out around the cluster of mountains; but they only sent out their herdsmen with their flocks to encroach gradually up the mountain slopes, and over the nearer vales, or drew the inhabitants towards them by the temptations and privileges of the abbeys and the castles. First, these Normans built Furness Abbey, on a plain to the south of the mountain group; and then between the mountains and the sea, Calder Abbey, to the west. Afterwards, they restored the religious house of St Bees, on the coast, and then a great Norman noble founded Lanercost Priory to the northeast. Thus they invested this noble fortress of nature – this mountain cluster – but they never took it. Their race at last mingled with the Saxon, and dwelt here as everywhere else, but it was by gradual penetration, and not by force or stratagem. The feudal retainers, sent to do service in tillage and herding became more and more free and independent of their lords, and as they became more free, they found easier access to the heart of the region, till, in course of time, they were in fact owners of portions of land, under a mere nominal subservience to the great men at a distance. This state of things is kept in mind by old customs at this day. I pay ninepence a year to Lord Lonsdale for my field, and am nominally his tenant, while my land is, to all practical purposes, freehold. The tenure is called Customary Freehold, and the nominal lord has no power when I have once acknowledged his old feudal claim by being 'made a tenant,' and paying my ninepence a year.

The holders of the crofts on the mountain sides, and in the vales (the inclosures built of stones, for the protection of the flocks from wild beasts, and for promoting the growth of the coppice on which they browsed), these tenants gradually becoming owners, were the original of the Dalesmen of our time. Since the union of Scotland with England, and the consequent extinction of border warfare, these dalesmen have become some of the quietest people in the world. No more summoned to war, nothing calls them out of their retreats, except an occasional market, or a sale of household furniture in some neighbouring valley. They go on practising their old-fashioned methods of tillage and herding, living in their primitive abodes, and keeping up customs, and even a manner of speech, which are elsewhere almost obsolete. It will not be so for long. Their agriculture cannot hold its ground against modern improvements. Their homespun linen and cloth do not answer now in comparison with Manchester cottons and Yorkshire woollens. Their sons part off to the manufacturing districts, to get a better maintenance than they can find at home; and the daughters must go out to service. Still, the old croft will not support those who remain; the land is mortgaged more deeply. The interest cannot be raised; and, under this pressure, the temptation to the sinking dalesman to drown his cares in drink, becomes too strong for many a one who has no resources of education to fall back upon. Then comes the end – the land and furniture are sold, the family disperse, and a stranger comes in who can make the land answer under modern methods of tillage. Some of these strangers have a sufficient love of what is consecrated by time, to retain as much as they can of the ancient character of the region, in the aspect of their dwellings, and the arrangement of their estates, but all cannot be expected to do this; and the antique air of the region must melt away. I have myself built a house of the graystone of the district, in the style of three centuries ago; but I see flaring white houses, square and modern, springing up in many a valley; and I feel that this time forward our West Moorlands will not lag behind the world – two or three centuries in the rear of adjoining counties – so charmingly as they have done from the dawn of British history till now.

As in many other mountain districts, the highest of our peaks are in the middle. Scawfell is the highest, and Bowfell the next, and they are nearly in the centre of the cluster. From this centre, not only do the ridges decline in height, but the valleys decrease in depth; so that on the outskirts, we have only gently sloping, green hills, and shallow vales, whence, in clear weather, we look up to the lofty central crags. In approaching from the south, through Lancashire, Windermere is the first of the lakes that is encountered. Gentle hills surround its southern end; and these rise and swell through the whole ten miles of its length, till, about its head, the diverging valleys are closed in by the heights of Fairfield, and the remarkable summits called the Langdale Pikes. Bowfell appears beyond them; and from some points on the lake, Scawfell itself is seen peeping over a nearer ridge. It was night when I arrived at the house of my host; and all that I knew of the road, for some miles, was that it was bordered by tufted walls, and overhung with trees, which on the left hand separated it from the lake. In the morning what a scene it was! The road was hidden, and the lawn before the windows seemed to slope down to the fringe of the trees, and the graceful little wooden promontory which jutted out into the lake. The gray waters spread out here about a mile in breadth. To the south they were lost among a group of wooded islands, while the head of the lake rounded off among green meadows, with here and there a rocky projection created with black pines, which were reflected in the waters below. A hamlet of white houses appeared in and out among the trees, at the foot of the rugged mountain, called Loughrigg, which separates the two diverging valleys at the head of Windermere. From my host's porch we looked up the quiet valley of the Brathay, where a beautiful little church, built by a mercer from Bond Street, crowns a wooded rock and overlooks the rattling river Brathay, to the glorious cluster of summits and ridges which the winter morning sun clothes with orange, crimson, and purple lines below where the snow cuts out a sharp outline against the sky. When I came to live here, I soon learned that if I wished for a calm, meditative walk after my morning's work, I had better go up this valley of the Brathay, where I was sure never to meet anybody. I could look out from its high churchyard upon its unsurpassed view, and then go down and skirt Loughrigg, and lean upon a gate, or rest upon a heathery perch of rock, without much probability of seeing a face for three hours together. Whereas, if I was tired of thinking, and sociably inclined, I had better take my way up the other valley – that of the Rotha, where the little town of Ambleside nestles under the shelter of the swelling Wansfell, and which is scattered over with dwellings throughout its circuit. In going round this valley, a walk of about five miles from my friend's house, it was pretty certain that we should meet the majority of our acquaintances on any fine winter afternoon. On going forth, the first thing that strikes the stranger's eye is probably the great abundance of evergreens. To me, the wintry aspect of the county is almost annihilated in the neighbourhood of dwellings, by the clustering and shining of the evergreens. The hollies in the hedges are tall and tree-like; and near the breakfast room windows of their houses, the inhabitants plant a holly to be an aviary in winter when birds come flitting about for the sake of the berries. Then the approaches are hedged in with laurels; the laurestina is in full flower on the lawns; the houses and walls are half covered with ivy; and wherever along the road, a garden wall stretches away, it runs over with evergreens, which shake off the snow as the breeze passes over them. Well, we go down the road to the toll-bar, where the good woman lives who likes her calling so well that she has no wish to leave her gate to see the world. She saw the world one afternoon for four hours, when her employer sent her to Bowness for a frolic; and she got so tired and dull that she was glad to see her toll-house again, and declared she would never more go pleasuring. I was in the boat with her that day – a packet-board steered by Professor Wilson, who had his friend Dr Blair with him. The contrast of the three faces was curious – the forlorn dullness of the woman, who looks the picture of content when taking a toll – the abstractions of the philological Dr Blair, and the keen, observing, and enjoying countenance of Christopher North! Just through the toll-bar, lies Waterhead, a cluster of houses on the northern margin of the lake, the prettiest of which is the low cottage under the massy sycamores, with its grass-plat spreading into the waters – the cottage where I lived while my house was building. Passing behind this cottage, the road winds somewhat inland, leaving space for a meadow between it and the lake, till it passes the Roman Camp before mentioned. Then on the right we see, across a field and almost hidden among evergreens, the cottage of poor Hartley Coleridge's tutor, the singular old clergyman who died at upwards of eighty, without a will, as if summoned untimely! Then we pass the beautiful house and most flowery garden of a Quaker friend of mine – a place which seems in all weathers to look as cheerful as its benevolent master. In my early walk, before it is light in the winter morning, I choose this direction in February, because in a copse of my Quaker friend's which overhangs the road there is always a more glorious tumult of singing-birds than in any other I know. To hear these birds on the one hand, and the gush of the rapid Rotha on the other, when the day is breaking over the waters, is enough to enliven the whole succeeding winter day. The

Rotha is here spanned by a bridge, which we must cross if we mean to go round the valley. We leave the highway now, and pass through a gate which makes the winding road half private for the whole time that we are skirting Loughrigg. Under wooded steeps and through copses we go, looking over the flat valley to the green swelling mountains on the other side, whose woods run down the ravines, and hang on the slopes, and peep out where the vales hide between. When I first came, there was a green knoll swelling up out of the meadows, under the opposite hills, with a chapel roof rising behind it; and a row of lowly graystone cottages near. When I first marked that knoll, I little thought that on it I should build my house, and that it would afford that terrace view which would be the daily delight of my life. But there now stands my graystone old English house, with climbing plants already half covering it, and a terrace wall below, inviting my fruit trees to spread themselves over it.

Our road now skirts the Rotha, a stream too clear to fish in, except after heavy rains. There is no beguiling the trout in water as translucent as the air. We do not now cross the little Millar Bridge, by which I am wont to go almost daily to Fox How; but we walk on to Fox How, through whose birch copse we have to pass. Everyone knows that Fox How is the abode so beloved by Dr Arnold – the house he built, and the garden he laid out to be the retreat of his old age. The trees that he planted spread and flourish, his house is almost covered with roses and climbing plants, his younger children are growing up there, and his friends assemble in his home; but he has long been gone. Perhaps there is not one of us that ever passes through that birch copse without vivid thoughts of him. As for me, I usually take my way through the garden, even if I have not time for more than a word at the window, or even for that. We now see the recess of Fairfield, its whole cul-de-sac, finely, unless mists are filling the basin, and curling about the ridges; and Rydal Forest stretches boldly up to the snow line. Lady Le Fleming's large, staring, yellow mansion is a blemish in the glorious view; but a little way back, we saw near it what puts all great mansions out of our heads – Wordsworth's cottage, a little way up the lower slope of Nab Scar – the blunt end of the Fairfield horseshoe. Of that cottage we must see more hereafter; it does not lie in our road now. After passing four or five dwellings, more or less prettily set down in their gardens, we come to Pelter Bridge, where we cross the Rotha again, and join the mail road. The river still sweeps beside us, among stones and under bending trees, joined here and there by a beck (brook) which has been making waterfalls in the ravines above. When we part company with it, we pass by more and more dwellings, one of the most striking of which, from its exquisite position on a hill-side is the large gray house built by the brother of Sir Humphry Davy. That gate is near my own. After passing both, and skirting the wall of Mr Harrison's grounds, we come to the little town of Ambleside. We had better pause at the foot of the hill leading up to the church; for we have more to say of Ambleside than we have room for here.

Emily Brontë, 'Loud Without the Wind Was Roaring', from *Poems, by Currer, Ellis, and Acton Bell* (1846)

Loud without the wind was roaring
Through th'autumnal sky;
Drenching wet, the cold rain pouring,
Spoke of winter nigh.
All too like that dreary eve,
Did my exiled spirit grieve.
Grieved at first, but grieved not long,
Sweet – how softly sweet! – it came;
Wild words of an ancient song,
Undefined, without a name.

'It was spring, and the skylark was singing:'
Those words, they awakened a spell;
They unlocked a deep fountain, whose springing,
Nor absence, nor distance can quell.

In the gloom of a cloudy November,
They uttered the music of May;
They kindled the perishing ember
Into fervour that could not decay.

Awaken o'er all my dear moorland,
West-wind in thy glory and pride!
Oh! call me from valley and lowland,
To walk by the hill-torrent's side!

It is swelled with the first snowy weather;
The rocks they are icy and hoar,
And sullenly waves the long heather,
And the fern leaves are sunny no more.

There are no yellow stars on the mountain
The bluebells have long died away
From the brink of the moss-bedded fountain –
From the side of the wintry brae.

But lovelier than corn-fields all waving
In emerald, and vermeil, and gold,
Are the heights where the north-wind is raving,
And the crags where I wandered of old.

It was morning: the bright sun was beaming;
How sweetly it brought back to me
The time when nor labour nor dreaming
Broke the sleep of the happy and free!

But blithely we rose as the dawn-heaven
Was melting to amber and blue.
And swift were the wings to our feet given,
While we traversed the meadows of dew.

For the moors! For the moors, where the short grass
Like velvet beneath us should lie!
For the moors! For the moors, where each high pass
Rose sunny against the clear sky!

For the moors, where the linnet was trilling
Its song on the old granite stone;
Where the lark, the wild sky-lark was filling
Every breast with delight like its own!

What language can utter the feeling
Which rose, when in exile afar,
On the brow of a lonely hill kneeling,
I saw the brown heath growing there?

It was scattered and stunted, and told me
That soon even that would be gone:
It whispered, 'The grim walls enfold me,
I have bloomed in my last summer's sun.'

But not the loved music, whose waking
Makes the soul of the Swiss die away,
Has a spell more adored and heartbreaking
Than, for me, in that blighted heath lay.

The spirit that bent 'neath its power,
How it longed – how it burned to be free!
If I could have wept in that hour,
Those tears had been heaven to me.

Well – well; the sad minutes are moving,
Though loaded with trouble and pain;
And some time the loved and the loving
Shall meet on the mountains again!

Emily Brontë, *Wuthering Heights* (1847)

Heathcliff lifted his hand, and the speaker sprang to a safer distance, obviously acquainted with its weight. Having no desire to be entertained by a cat-and-dog combat, I stepped forward briskly, as if eager to partake of the warmth of the hearth, and innocent of any knowledge of the interrupted dispute. Each had enough decorum to suspend further hostilities: Heathcliff placed his fists, out of temptation, in his pockets; Mrs Heathcliff curled her lip, and walked to a seat far off, where she kept her word by playing the part of a statue during the remainder of my stay. That was not long. I declined joining their breakfast, and, at the first gleam of dawn, took an opportunity of escaping into the free air, now clear, and still, and cold as impalpable ice.

My landlord hallooed for me to stop, ere I reached the bottom of the garden, and offered to accompany me across the moor. It was well he did, for the whole hill-back was one billowy, white ocean; the swells and falls not indicating corresponding rises and depressions in the ground: many pits, at least, were filled to a level; and entire ranges of mounds, the refuse of the quarries, blotted from the chart which my yesterday's walk left pictured in my mind. I had remarked on one side of the road, at intervals of six or seven yards, a line of upright stones, continued through the whole length of the barren: these were erected, and daubed with lime on purpose to serve as guides in the dark; and also when a fall, like the present, confounded the deep swamps on either hand with the firmer path: but, excepting a dirty dot pointing up here and there, all traces of their existence had vanished: and my companion found it necessary to warn me frequently to steer to the right or left, when I imagined I was following, correctly, the windings of the road. We exchanged little conversation, and he halted at the entrance of Thrushcross Park, saying I could make no error there. Our adieux were limited to a hasty bow, and then I pushed forward, trusting to my own resources; for the porter's lodge is untenanted as yet. The distance from the gate to the Grange is two miles: I believe I managed to make it four; what with losing myself among the trees, and sinking up to the neck in snow: a predicament which only those who have experienced it can appreciate. At any rate, whatever my wanderings, the clock chimed twelve as I entered the house; and that gave exactly an hour for every mile of the usual way from Wuthering Heights.

Harriet Martineau to Mr H. G. Atkinson, 7 November 1847, from *Autobiography*

I always go out before it is quite light; and in the fine mornings I go up the hill behind the church, – the Kirkstone road, – where I reach a great height, and see from half way along Windermere to Rydal. When the little shred of moon that is left, and the morning star, hang over Wansfell, among the amber clouds of the approaching sunrise, it is delicious. On the positively rainy mornings, my walk is to Pelter Bridge and back. Sometimes it is round the south end of the valley. These early walks (I sit down to breakfast at half-past seven) are good, among other things, in preparing me in mind for my work. It is *very serious* work.

Christina Rossetti, 'The Trees' Counselling' (1847)

I was strolling sorrowfully
   Thro' the corn fields and the meadows;
The stream sounded melancholy,
   And I walked among the shadows;
While the ancient forest trees
Talked together in the breeze;
In the breeze that waved and blew them,
With a strange weird rustle thro' them.

Said the oak unto the others
   In a leafy voice and pleasant:
'Here we all are equal brothers,
   'Here we have nor lord nor peasant.
'Summer, Autumn, Winter, Spring,
'Pass in happy following.
'Little winds may whistle by us,
'Little birds may overfly us;

'But the sun still waits in heaven
   'To look down on us in splendour;
'When he goes the moon is given,
   'Full of rays that he doth lend her:
'And tho' sometimes in the night
'Mists may hide her from our sight,
'She comes out in the calm weather,
'With the glorious stars together.'

From the fruitage, the blossom,
   From the trees came no denying;
Then my heart said in my bosom:
   'Wherefore art thou sad and sighing?
'Learn contentment from this wood
'That proclaimeth all states good;
'Go not from it as it found thee;
'Turn thyself and gaze around thee.'

And I turned: behold the shading
   But showed forth the light more clearly;
The wild bees were honey-lading;
   The stream sounded hushing merely,
And the wind not murmuring
Seemed, but gently whispering:
'Get thee patience; and thy spirit
'Shall discern in all things merit.'

'Often Rebuked, yet Always Back Returning', from *Wuthering Heights* and *Agnes Grey*, ed. Charlotte Brontë (1850)

Charlotte or Emily Brontë

Often rebuked, yet always back returning
    To those first feelings that were born with me,
And leaving busy chase of wealth and learning
    For idle dreams of things which cannot be:

To-day, I will seek not the shadowy region;
    Its unsustaining vastness waxes drear;
And visions rising, legion after legion,
    Bring the unreal world too strangely near.

I'll walk, but not in old heroic traces,
    And not in paths of high morality,
And not among the half-distinguished faces,
    The clouded forms of long-past history.

I'll walk where my own nature would be leading:
    It vexes me to choose another guide:
Where the grey flocks in ferny glades are feeding;
    Where the wild wind blows on the mountain side.

What have those lonely mountains worth revealing?
    More glory and more grief than I can tell:
The earth that wakes *one* human heart to feeling
    Can centre both the worlds of Heaven and Hell.

Harriet Martineau, *A Complete Guide to the English Lakes* (1855)

The stranger has now made his three tours. There is one thing more that he must do before he goes on into Cumberland. He must spend a day on the Mountains: and if alone, so much the better. If he knows what it is to spend a day so far above the every-day world, he is aware that it is good to be alone (unless there is danger in the case); and, if he is a novice, let him try whether it be not so. Let him go forth early, with a stout stick in his hand, provision for the day in his knapsack or his pocket; and, if he chooses, a book: but we do not think he will read to-day. A map is essential, to explain to him what he sees: and it is very well to have a pocket compass, in case of sudden fog, or any awkward doubt about the way. In case of an ascent of a formidable mountain, like Scawfell or Helvellyn, it is rash to go without a guide: but our tourist shall undertake something more moderate, and reasonably safe, for a beginning.

What mountain shall it be? He might go up Blackcombe, on his way to or from Furness: and from thence he might see, in fair weather, as Wordsworth tells us, 'a more extensive view than from any other point in Britain,' – seven English counties, and seven Scotch, a good deal of Wales, the Isle of Man, and in some lucky moment, just before sunrise (as the Ordnance surveyors say) the coast of Ireland. This is very fine; but it is hardly what is looked for in the lake district, – the sea being the main feature. He might go up the Old Man of Coniston; but there are the copper works, and there is the necessity of a guide: and it is a long way to go for the day's treat. If he ascends the Langdale Pikes, it had better be from some interior station; and the rest of the great peaks will be best commanded from Keswick. Of those within reach of Ambleside, which shall it be? Loughrigg is very easy and very charming; but it is not commanding enough. From the surrounding heights it looks like a mere rambling hill. Wansfell is nearest, and also easy and safe. It may be reached from a charming walk from Low Wood Inn, and descended by the Stockghyll lane, above Ambleside. The immediate neighbourhood is mapped out below; and there is a long and wide opening to the south: but to the north-east, and everywhere round the head of the lake, the view is stopped, first by Nab Scar, and then by other heights. Why should it not be Nab Scar itself? or, the whole of Fairfield? That excursion is safe, not over-fatiguing, practicable for a summer day, and presenting scenery as characteristic as can be found. Let it be Fairfield.

The stranger should ascend to the ridge, either through Rydal forest (for which leave is requisite, and not always easily obtained,) or by the road to the Nook which anybody will shew him. The Nook is a farmhouse in a glorious situation, as he will see when he gets there and steps into the field on the left, to look abroad from the brow. He then passes under its old trees to where the voice of falling waters calls him onward. Scandale Beck comes tumbling down its rocky channel, close at hand. He must cross the bridge, and follow the cart-road, which brings him out at once upon the fells. What he has to aim at is the ridge above Rydal forest or park, from whence his way is plain, – round the whole *cul-de-sac* of Fairfield, to Nab Scar. He sees it all; and the only thing is to do it: and we know of no obstacle to his doing it, unless it be the stone wall which divides the Scandale from the Rydal side of the ridge. These stone walls are an inconvenience to pedestrians, and a great blemish in the eyes of strangers. In the first place, however, it is to be said that an open way is almost invariably left, up every mountain, if the rover can but find it; and, in the next place, the ugliness of these climbing fences disappears marvellously when the stranger learns how they come there. – In the olden times, when there were wolves, and when the abbots of the surrounding Norman monasteries encouraged their tenants to approach nearer and nearer to the Saxon fastnesses, the shepherds were allowed to inclose crofts about their upland huts, for the sake of browsing their flocks on the sprouts of the ash and the holly with which the hillsides were then wooded, and of protecting the sheep from the wolves which haunted the thickets. The inclosures certainly spread up the mountain sides, at this day, to a height where they would not be seen if ancient custom had not drawn the lines which are thus preserved; and it appears, from historical testimony, that these fences existed before the fertile valleys were portioned out among many holders. Higher and higher ran these stone inclosures, – threading the woods, and joining on upon the rocks. Now, the woods are for the most part gone; and the walls offend and perplex the stranger's eye and mind by their unsightliness and apparent uselessness; but it is a question whether, their

origin once known, they would be willingly parted with, –
reminding us as they do of the times when the tenants of the
abbots or military nobles formed a link between the new race
of inhabitants and the Saxon remnant of the old. One of these
walls it is which runs along the ridge and bounds Rydal Park.
There may be a gate in it; or one which enables the stranger
to get round it. If not, he must go over it; and if he does so,
high enough up, it may save him another climb. The nearer the
ridge, the fewer the remaining walls between him and liberty.
Once in the forest, Christopher North's advice comes into
his mind, – unspoiled by the fear, only too reasonable in the
lower part of the park, – of being turned out of the paradise,
very summarily. 'The sylvan, or rather, the forest scenery of
Rydal Park,' says Professor Wilson, 'was, in the memory of
living man, magnificent; and it still contains a treasure of old
trees. By all means wander away into these old woods, and lose
yourself for an hour or two among the cooing of cushats and
the shrill shriek of startled blackbirds, and the rustle of the
harmless glow-worm among the last year's beech leaves. No
very great harm should you even fall asleep under the shadow
of an oak, whilst the magpie chatters at safe distance, and the
more innocent squirrel peeps down upon you from a bough of
the canopy, and then, hoisting his tail, glides into the obscurity
of the loftiest umbrage.' – Ascending from these shades through
a more straggling woodland, the stranger arrives at a clump
on the ridge, – the last clump, and thenceforth feels himself
wholly free. His foot is on the springy mountain moss; and
many a cushion of heather tempts him to sit down and look
abroad. There may still be a frightened cow or two, wheeling
away, with tails aloft, as he comes onwards; and a few sheep

are still crouching in the shadows of the rocks, or staring at him from the knolls. If he plays the child and bleats, he will soon see how many there are. It is one of the amusements of a good mimic in such places to bring about him all the animals there are, by imitating their cries. One may assemble a flock of sheep, and lead them far out of bounds in this way; and bewildered enough they look when the bleat ceases, and they are left to find their way back again. It is in such places as this that the truth of some of Wordsworth's touches may be recognised, which are most amusing to cockney readers. Perhaps no passage has been more ridiculed than that which tells of the 'solemn bleat' of

'a lamb left somewhere to itself,

The plaintive spirit of the solitude.'

The laughers are thinking of a cattle market, or a flock of sheep on a dusty road; and they know nothing of the effect of a single bleat of a stray lamb high up on the mountains. If they had ever felt the profound stillness of the higher fells, or heard it broken by the plaintive cry, repeated and not answered, they would be aware that there is a true solemnity in the sound.

Still further on, when the sheep are all left behind, he may see a hawk perched upon a great boulder. He will see it take flight when he comes near, and cleave the air below him, and hang above the woods, – to the infinite terror, as he knows, of many a small creature there, and then whirl away to some distant part of the park. Perhaps a heavy buzzard may rise, flapping, from its nest on the moor, or pounce from a crag in the direction of any water-birds that may be about the springs and pools in the hills. There is no other sound, unless it be the hum of the gnats in the hot sunshine. There is an aged man in the district, however, who hears more than this, and sees more than people below would, perhaps, imagine. An old shepherd has the charge of four rain gauges which are set up on four ridges, – desolate, misty spots, sometimes below and often above the clouds. He visits each once a month, and notes down what these gauges record; and when the tall old man, with his staff, passes out of sight into the cloud, or among the cresting rocks, it is a striking thought that science has set up a tabernacle in these wildernesses, and found a priest among the shepherds. That old man has seen and heard wonderful things: – has trod upon rainbows, and been waited upon by a dim retinue of spectral mists. He has seen the hail and the lightnings go forth as from under his hand, and has stood in the sunshine, listening to the thunder growling, and the tempest bursting beneath his feet. He well knows the silence of the hills, and all the solemn ways in which that silence is broken. The stranger, however, coming hither on a calm summer day, may well fancy that a silence like this can never be broken.

Looking abroad, what does he see? The first impression probably is of the billowy character of the mountain groups around and below him. This is perhaps the most striking feature of such a scene to a novice; and the next is the flitting character of the mists. One ghostly peak after another seems to rise out of its shroud; and then the shroud winds itself round another. Here the mist floats over a valley; there it reeks out of a chasm: here it rests upon a green slope; there it curls up a black precipice. The sunny vales below look like a paradise, with their bright meadows and waters and shadowy woods, and little knots of villages. To the south there is the glittering sea; and the estuaries of the Leven and Duddon, with their

stretches of yellow sands. To the east there is a sea of hill tops.
On the north, Ullswater appears, grey and calm at the foot
of black precipices; and nearer may be traced the whole pass
from Patterdale, where Brothers' Water lies invisible from
hence. The finest point of the whole excursion is about the
middle of the *cul-de-sac*, where, on the northern sides, there
are tremendous precipices, overlooking Deepdale, and other
sweet recesses far below. Here, within hearing of the torrents
which tumble from those precipices, the rover should rest. He
will see nothing so fine as the contrast of this northern view
with the long green slope on the other side, down to the source
of Rydal Beck, and then down and down to Rydal Woods
and Mount. He is now 2,950 feet above the sea level; and he
has surely earned his meal. If the wind troubles him, he can
doubtless find a sheltered place under a rock. If he can sit on
the bare ridge, he is the more fortunate.

The further he goes, the more amazed he is at the extent
of the walk, which looked such a trifle from below. Waking
out of a reverie, an hour after dinner, he sees that the sun is
some way down the western sky. He hastens on, not heeding
the boggy spaces, and springing along the pathless heather and
moss, seeing more and more lakes and tarns every quarter of
an hour. In the course of the day he sees ten. Windermere,
and little Blelham Tarn beyond, he saw first. Ullswater was
below him to the north when he dined; and, presently after,
a tempting path guided his eye to Grisedale Tarn lying in the
pass from Patterdale to Grasmere. Here are four. Next, comes
Grasmere, with Easedale Tarn above it, in its mountain hollow:
then Rydal, of course, at its feet; and Elterwater beyond the
western ridges; and finally, to the south-west, Esthwaite Water

and Coniston. There are the ten. Eight of these may be seen at once from at least one point – Nab Scar, whence he must take his last complete survey; for from hence he must plunge down the steep slope, and bid farewell to all that lies behind the ridge. The day has gone like an hour. The sunshine is leaving the surface of the nearer lakes, and the purple bloom of the evening is on the further mountains; and the gushes of yellow light between the western passes shows that sunset is near. He must hasten down, – mindful of the opening between the fences, which he remarked from below, and which, if he finds, he cannot lose his way. He does not seriously lose his way, though crag and bog make him diverge now and then. Descending between the inclosures, he sits down once or twice, to relieve the fatigue to the ancle and instep of so continuous a descent, and to linger a little over the beauty of the evening scene. As he comes down into the basin where Rydal Beck makes its last gambols and leaps, before entering the park, he is sensible of the approach of night. Loughrigg seems to rise: the hills seem to close him in, and the twilight to settle down. He comes to a gate, and finds himself in the civilised world again. He descends the green lane at the top of Rydal Mount, comes out just above Wordsworth's gate, finds his car at the bottom of the hill, – (the driver beginning to speculate on whether any accident has befallen the gentleman on the hills,) – is driven home, and is amazed, on getting out, to find how stiff and tired he is. He would not, however, but have spent such a day for ten times the fatigue. He will certainly ascend Helvellyn, and every other mountain that comes in his way.

Elizabeth Barrett Browning, *Aurora Leigh* (1856)

And I, who spoke the truth then, stand upright,
Still worthy of having spoken out the truth,
By being content I spoke it though it set
Him there, me here. – O woman's vile remorse,
To hanker after a mere name, a show,
A supposition, a potential love!
Does every man who names love in our lives
Become a power for that? is love's true thing
So much best to us, that what personates love
Is next best? A potential love, forsooth!
We are not so vile. No, no – he cleaves, I think,
This man, this image, . . . chiefly for the wrong
And shock he gave my life, in finding me
Precisely where the devil of my youth
Had set me, on those mountain-peaks of hope
All glittering with the dawn-dew, all erect
And famished for the morning, – saying, while
I looked for empire and much tribute, 'Come,
I have some worthy work for thee below.
Come, sweep my barns and keep my hospitals,
And I will pay thee with a current coin

Which men give women.'
                              As we spoke, the grass
Was trod in haste beside us, and my aunt,
With smile distorted by the sun, – face, voice,
As much at issue with the summer-day
As if you brought a candle out of doors,
Broke in with 'Romney, here! – My child, entreat
Your cousin to the house, and have your talk,
If girls must talk upon their birthdays. Come.'

He answered for me calmly, with pale lips
That seemed to motion for a smile in vain.
'The talk is ended, madam, where we stand.
Your brother's daughter has dismissed me here;
And all my answer can be better said
Beneath the trees, than wrong by such a word
Your house's hospitalities. Farewell.'

With that he vanished. I could hear his heel
Ring bluntly in the lane, as down her leapt
The short way from us. – Then a measured speech
Withdrew me. 'What means this, Aurora Leigh?
My brother's daughter has dismissed my guests?'

The lion in me felt the keeper's voice,
Through all its quivering dewlaps: I was quelled
Before her, – meekened to the child she knew:
I prayed her pardon, said, 'I had little thought
To give dismissal to a guest of hers,
In letting go a friend of mine, who came

To take me into service as a wife, –
No more than that, indeed.'
                              'No more, no more?
Pray heaven,' she answered, 'that I was not mad.
I could not mean to tell her to her face
That Romney Leigh had asked me for a wife,
And I refused him?'

                              'Did he ask?' I said;
'I think he rather stooped to take me up
For certain uses which he found to do
For something called a wife. He never asked.'

'What stuff!' she answered; 'are they queens, these girls?
That must have mantles, stitched with twenty silks,
Spread out upon the ground, before they'll step
One footstep for the noblest lover born.'

'But I am born,' I said with firmness, 'I,
To walk another way than his, dear aunt.'

'You walk, you walk! A babe at thirteen months
Will walk as well as you,' she cried in haste,
'Without a steadying finger. Why, you child,
God help you, you are groping in the dark,
For all this sunlight. You suppose, perhaps,
That you, sole offspring of an opulent man,
Are rich and free to choose which way to walk?
You think, and it's a reasonable thought,
That I besides, being well to do in life,

Will leave my handful in my niece's hand
When death shall paralyse these fingers? Pray,
Pray, child, albeit I know you love me not,
As if you loved me, that I may not die!
For when I die and leave you, out you go,
(Unless I make room for you in my grave),
Unhoused, unfed, my dear poor brother's lamb,
(Ah heaven! – that pains!) – without a right to crop
A single blade of grass beneath these trees,
Or cast a lamb's small shadow on the lawn,
Unfed, unfolded!

Charlotte Brontë, *The Professor* (1857)

A fine October Morning succeeded to the foggy evening that had witnessed my first introduction to Crimsworth-Hall. I was early up and walking in the large, park-like meadow surrounding the house. The autumn sun, rising over the — shire hills, disclosed a pleasant country; woods brown and mellow varied the fields from which the harvest had been lately carried; a river, gliding between the woods, caught on its surface the somewhat cold gleam of the October sun and sky: at frequent intervals along the banks of the river – tall, cylindrical chimnies, almost like slender, round towers, indicated the factories which the trees half concealed; here and there mansions, similar to Crimsworth-Hall, occupied agreeable sites on the hill-side; the country wore, on the whole, a cheerful, active, fertile look – Steam, Trade, Machinery had long banished from it all romance and seclusion. At a distance of five miles – a valley, opening between the low hills, held in its cup the great town of X—; a dense, permanent vapour brooded over this locality – there lay Edward's 'Concern'.

I forced my eye to scrutinise this prospect, I forced my mind to dwell on it for a time, and when I found that it communicated no pleasurable emotion to my heart – that it stirred in me none of the hopes a man ought to feel when he sees laid before him the scene of his life's career – I said to myself, 'William – you are a rebel against circumstances; you are a fool and know not what you want – you have chosen trade and you shall be a tradesman; look!' I continued mentally, 'Look at the sooty smoke in that hollow and know that there is your post! There you cannot dream, you cannot speculate and theorize – there you shall out and work!'

Thus self-schooled, I returned to the house.

Eliza Keary, 'Through the Wood', from *Little Seal-Skin* (1874)

Outside,
A world in sunshine;
Upon an afternoon
Once in June.
Such a wide,
Deep light-flooding, we were almost
Drowned in it where we stood,
Nellie and I; but inside the Wood
Clean stems grew close to each other; overhead
The intertwined light branches threw
Sweet shade on the rough ground.
I said, 'Nellie,
Let us walk into the tall Wood.'
She, putting her hand in mine,
Led me on softly, and so replied.
We made the only sound that there was,
With our footsteps crushing
The light tumble of leaves on scant grass;
Not the ghost of a bird's song under
Any cover of bush.
So along and along

We went, pushing
Our way where the tangled wood came,
Neither inclined for talking. As for me,
It was all I wanted, to walk by Nellie;
And she – . O! no blame
To the rapt wonder in her face.
This was Nellie –
The great silent glory
Of the beautiful day
Had found a place that he could stay
In – Nellie –
And wrote her through with his story.
So she passed on silently,
Walking by me,
Heaven's temple by me.
Heaven is full of love,
I thought, over and over,
And said to my heart, 'Hush!
You are happy, certainly.'
Just then, from above,
Came three notes of a thrush,
Satisfied, low, out of a full breast;
Then Nellie broke silence, and said,
'You know we shall part presently, you and I,
At the end of the Wood. Friend,
I've a favour to ask of you; –
I may call you friend, and won't tell
A long tale; one word's best.
This little packet – well,
Give it to Robert,

Into his own hand.
Thank you. He will understand.
I knew you wouldn't mind it for me.
You're not hurt?'
'I – Oh, no!' I understood.
After that, silently,
We walked on to the end of the Wood.

***

Outside,
A world in sunshine;
She with her hand in mine:
Such a wide, dark flood;
I died in it, where I stood –
By the side of Nellie.

Kate Chopin, 'Beyond the Bayou' (1893)

The first touch of the cool gray morning awoke La Folle. She arose, calmly, as if no tempest had shaken and threatened her existence but yesterday.

She donned her new blue cottonade and white apron, for she remembered that this was Sunday. When she had made for herself a cup of strong black coffee, and drunk it with relish, she quitted the cabin and walked across the old familiar field to the bayou's edge again.

She did not stop there as she had always done before, but crossed with a long, steady stride as if she had done this all her life.

When she had made her way through the brush and scrub-cottonwood trees that lined the opposite bank, she found herself upon the border of a field where the white, bursting cotton, with the dew upon it, gleamed for acres and acres like frosted silver in the early dawn.

La Folle drew a long, deep breath as she gazed across the country. She walked slowly and uncertainly, like one who hardly knows how, looking about her as she went.

The cabins, that yesterday had sent a clamor of voices to pursue her, were quiet now. No one was yet astir at Belissime.

Only the birds that darted here and there from hedges were awake, and singing their matins.

When La Folle came to the broad stretch of velvety lawn that surrounded the house, she moved slowly and with delight over the springy turf that was delicious beneath her tread. More and more slowly she went, with clear senses and fear dead, and joy at her heart.

She stopped to find whence came those perfumes that were stealing over her with memories from a time far gone.

Sweet odors swooned to her from the thousand blue violets that peeped out from green, luxuriant beds. Fragrance showered down from the big waxen bells of the magnolias far above her head, and from the jessamine clumps around her.

There were roses, too, without number. To right and left palms spread in broad and graceful curves. It all looked like enchantment beneath the sparkling sheen of dew.

When La Folle had slowly and cautiously mounted the many steps that led up to the veranda, she turned to look back at the perilous ascent she had made. Now she caught sight of the river, bending like a silver bow at the foot of Bellissime. Exultation possessed her soul. All the world was fair about her, and green and white and blue and silvery shinings had come again instead of that frightful fancy of interminable red!

Gwen John to Ursula Tyrwhitt,
3 September 1903, La Réole

I was interrupted yesterday by a man who passed in a great *charette*, he shouted that he would take us to the next village so we had to bundle our things in and get in as every lift seems saving of time and therefore money too so we always take them – last week we travelled in a motor car – not all the week! But one day – till it broke down. The man in the *charette* was quite charming and took us a long way, we got down at the village when it was dark and went into the inn – into an immense deserted room – it did not look promising for work, till at last the woman laid a long table for many people so we waited till they came in. The village street looked so beautiful in the evening light, there were beautiful trees in it and antique houses. When the men came in they made so great a row that we went into the street, till they had finished dinner. We asked the woman first if she would let us a room and she said she had not got one, which was a lie, we walked up and down the street singing, to practice singing as sometimes they want us to and then we tried to get a room, but they did not like us in that village, they thought us *mauvais sujets*, they asked us 2 francs for one place which is absurd. We only sleep in on rare occasions, when we work late for then it is rather dangerous to set out, they want to know where we are going to sleep and follow us. When we came back we showed our specimens and began to draw the men who would pose. They criticized our drawings so much that I asked one of them if he was an artist. He said 'a sculptor' and that there were many painters in the room – I said '*tant pis pour nous*' and he said '*non, non, tant mieux*', then the artist gave us a lesson and indeed what they said did me a lot of good. They talked about my lines being too short, how we must draw the long lines first etc. – of course my drawing and everybody's, I suppose, gradually gets less choppy, but it is good to have things pointed out. We left in haste and fear and indignation, the people were so boisterous. And what do you think the woman charged: 2 francs for our dinner and we had hardly anything – I called her a thief twice, I was in a temper. We were followed by two men and one was the *charette* man to whom I spoke like an angel and so touched his heart so he left us after we had promised to meet him in La Réole. I was glad to shake the dust of that village off my feet, we did not earn 1.50 and we spent 2 francs there! We were so tired we slept in the first place at all secluded. There was no moon but the sky was covered with stars. Before we went to sleep we had to approach a terrible-looking thing which made a strange noise every now and then. It looked to me like a gigantic hearse with black phantoms sitting in it. We were so frightened but it turned out to be some kind of engine whose machinery made that noise every now and then. We slept under some haystacks. In the morning I was awakened by Dorelia saying there was a man looking at us – I was so sleepy I did not care if the whole world was looking at me sleeping. We had little congregations for hours, they always wake me up by saying something – they are not considerate. Dorelia is always awake, I, when I wake, I pretend generally to be asleep because I am too sleepy to talk to them.

I have been interrupted again and many things have happened. La Réole was unsympathetic one night and four nights ago we came to a little village where we worked a great deal and there was a beautiful woman there who kept the inn – she was young and intensely interesting, she took an affection for us. But things turned out badly again for us, because they could not make us out enough, she thought again we were bad girls, so she would not have us live with her as she wanted – nor her husband, and some nights after we were frightfully hungry and tired and in a different part of the country – miles away, the people were very inhospitable, we went into a house where they were having dinner, they would not sell us bread. I called them savages, that hurt them and they came all running after us calling out they were not savages and offering us bread, but we would not stop of course and after some time we were overtaken by a young man, and we talked to him and then with him we got some bread at a house, and then we walked with him to this town, Meilhan – or rather near to it where we had hidden our baggage in a wood, and he turned out to be a loved of that beautiful woman Madeleine Latapi before she was married, so we could send messages to her. When we were by ourselves again we came to a bridge and a flock of sheep and an old man. The old man told us not to cross the bridge which we meant to do, but he conducted us down a side path and made us walk with him along a road, we walked very fast so that the sheep might be left behind and then he would have to stay too, but whenever the sheep got far behind he said something and they all ran as fast as anything up to him. It was a very dark night so we could not see his face, he could not speak much French, only the patois. We were so tired but he would not let us stop a minute. At last we came to his house and he tried to make us come in for a bit, he was really a very nice old man, but we declined and then he shook hands. When he had shaken hands we knew who he was by his hand, he had no little finger and two of the others were bent up, so we knew he was an old man we had drawn in an inn and drank beer with, and lemonade. It gave us rather a horrid sensation. It was so dark when we got near the place we had hidden our things we could not find them – we were so tired that we sat down on a slanting place of stones, slanting down to the river, and I went to sleep even, now and then, the cold was so frightful, it was a night of real misery – Dorelia did not sleep at all and my sleep was more like a waking nightmare, we lay on each other to feel a little warmer and covered ourselves with our portfolios, but the stones were like ice. When it was light we found our baggage and went to sleep on the side of the road because we were too sleepy to move another step away. When we were sleeping some people from the town came and saw us, everybody knows here that we slept out. This is a beautiful place, large and built on a hill – the people are sympathetic, *quelque part*. They give us work and food and flowers, they gave us a beautiful stable to sleep in. People come to look at us in the stable, a young artist who gave us his address in Paris, so that we can be models if we like in Paris.

I cannot write any more now, as two *mauvais sujets* are sitting by us and will not go away. Write to me at Agen to the *poste restante*. I wear your little charm.

Yours with much love,

Gwen

Katherine Mansfield, *Journal of Katherine Mansfield*, Sunday, 16 May 1915

Paris. I dreamed all night of Rupert Brooke. And to-day as I left the house he was standing at the door, with rucksack on his back and his hat shading his face. So after I had posted J.'s letter I did not go home. I went a long, very idle sort of amble along the quais. It was exquisitely hot: white clouds lay upon the sky like sheets spread out to dry. On the big sand-heaps down by the river children had hollowed out tunnels and caverns. They sat in them, stolid and content, their hair glistening in the sun. Now and then a man lay stretched on his face, his head in his arms. The river was full of big silver stars; the trees shook, faintly glinting with light. I found delightful places – little squares with white square houses. Quite hollow they looked, with the windows gaping open. Narrow streets arched over the chestnut boughs, or perhaps quite deserted, with a clock tower showing over the roofs. The sun put a spell on everything.

I crossed and recrossed the river and leaned over the bridges and kept thinking we were coming to a park when we weren't. You cannot think what a pleasure my invisible, imaginary companion gave me. If he had been alive it would never have possibly occurred; but – it's a game I like to play – to walk and talk with the dead who smile and are silent, and *free*, quite finally free.

Virginia Woolf, *Mrs Dalloway* (1925)

For having lived in Westminster – how many years now? over twenty, – one feels even in the midst of the traffic, or waking at night, Clarissa was positive, a particular hush, or solemnity; an indescribable pause; a suspense (but that might be her heart, affected, they said, by influenza) before Big Ben strikes. There! Out it boomed. First a warning, musical; then the hour, irrevocable. The leaden circles dissolved in the air. Such fools we are, she thought, crossing Victoria Street. For Heaven only knows why one loves it so, how one sees it so, making it up, building it round one, tumbling it, creating it every moment afresh; but the veriest frumps, the most dejected of miseries sitting on doorsteps (drink their downfall) do the same; can't be dealt with, she felt positive, by Acts of Parliament for that very reason: they love life. In people's eyes, in the swing, tramp, and trudge; in the bellow and the uproar; the carriages, motor cars, omnibuses, vans, sandwich men shuffling and swinging; brass bands; barrel organs; in the triumph and the jingle and the strange high singing of some aeroplane overhead was what she loved; life; London; this moment in June.

For it was the middle of June. The War was over, except for some one like Mrs Foxcroft at the Embassy last night eating her heart out because that nice boy was killed and now the old Manor House must go to a cousin; or Lady Bexborough who opened a bazaar, they said, with the telegram in her hand, John, her favourite, killed; but it was over; thank Heaven – over. It was June. The King and Queen were at the Palace. And everywhere, though it was still so early, there was a beating, a stirring of galloping ponies, tapping of cricket bats; Lords, Ascot, Ranelagh and all the rest of it; wrapped in the soft mesh of the grey-blue morning air, which, as the day wore on, would unwind them, and set down on their lawns and pitches the bouncing ponies, whose forefeet just struck the ground and up they sprung, the whirling young men, and laughing girls in their transparent muslins who, even now, after dancing all night, were taking their absurd woolly dogs for a run; and even now, at this hour, discreet old dowagers were shooting out in their motor cars on errands of mystery; and the shopkeepers were fidgeting in their windows with their paste and diamonds, their lovely old sea-green brooches in eighteenth-century settings to tempt Americans (but one must economise, not buy things rashly for Elizabeth), and she, too, loving it as she did with an absurd and faithful passion, being part of it, since her people were courtiers once in the time of the Georges, she, too, was going that very night to kindle and illuminate; to give her party. But how strange, on entering the Park, the silence; the mist; the hum; the slow-swimming happy ducks; the pouched birds waddling; and who should be coming along with his back against the Government buildings, most appropriately, carrying a despatch box stamped with the Royal Arms, who but Hugh Whitbread; her old friend Hugh – the admirable Hugh!

'Good-morning to you, Clarissa!' said Hugh, rather extravagantly, for they had known each other as children. 'Where are you off to?'

'I love walking in London,' said Mrs. Dalloway. 'Really, it's better than walking in the country.'

Virginia Woolf, *Street Haunting: A London Adventure* (1927)

In these minutes in which a ghost has been sought for, a quarrel composed, and a pencil bought, the streets had become completely empty. Life had withdrawn to the top floor, and lamps were lit. The pavement was dry and hard; the road was of hammered silver. Walking home through the desolation one could tell oneself the story of the dwarf, of the blind men, of the party in the Mayfair mansion, of the quarrel in the stationer's shop. Into each of these lives one could penetrate a little way, far enough to give oneself the illusion that one is not tethered to a single mind, but can put on briefly for a few minutes the bodies and minds of others. One could become a washerwoman, a publican, a street singer. And what greater delight and wonder can there be than to leave the straight lines of personality and deviate into those footpaths that lead beneath brambles and thick tree trunks into the heart of the forest where live those wild beasts, our fellow men?

Virginia Woolf, *To the Lighthouse* (1927)

She had a dull errand in the town; she had a letter or two to write; she would be ten minutes perhaps; she would put on her hat. And, with her basket and her parasol, there she was again, ten minutes later, giving out a sense of being ready, of being equipped for a jaunt, which, however, she must interrupt for a moment, as they passed the tennis lawn, to ask Mr Carmichael, who was basking with his yellow cat's eyes ajar, so that like a cat's they seemed to reflect the branches moving or the clouds passing, but to give no inkling of any inner thoughts or emotion whatsoever, if he wanted anything.

For they were making the great expedition, she said, laughing. They were going to the town. 'Stamps, writing-paper, tobacco?' she suggested, stopping by his side. But no, he wanted nothing. His hands clasped themselves over his capacious paunch, his eyes blinked, as if he would have liked to reply kindly to these blandishments (she was seductive but a little nervous) but could not, sunk as he was in a grey-green somnolence which embraced them all, without need of words, in a vast and benevolent lethargy of well-wishing; all the house; all the world; all the people in it, for he had slipped into his glass at lunch a few drops of something, which accounted, the children thought, for the vivid streak of canary-yellow in moustache and beard that were otherwise milk white. He wanted nothing, he murmured.

He should have been a great philosopher, said Mrs Ramsay, as they went down the road to the fishing village, but he had made an unfortunate marriage. Holding her black parasol very erect, and moving with an indescribable air of expectation, as if she were going to meet someone round the corner, she told the story; an affair at Oxford with some girl; an early marriage; poverty; going to India; translating a little poetry 'very beautifully, I believe,' being willing to teach the boys Persian or Hindustanee, but what really was the use of that? – and then lying, as they saw him, on the lawn.

It flattered him; snubbed as he had been, it soothed him that Mrs Ramsay should tell him this. Charles Tansley revived. Insinuating, too, as she did the greatness of man's intellect, even in its decay, the subjection of all wives – not that she blamed the girl, and the marriage had been happy enough, she believed – to their husband's labours, she made him feel better pleased with himself than he had done yet, and he would have liked, had they taken a cab, for example, to have paid the fare. As for her little bag, might he not carry that? No, no, she said, she always carried *that* herself. She did too. Yes, he felt that in her. He felt many things, something in particular that excited him and disturbed him for reasons which he could not give. He would like her to see him, gowned and hooded, walking in a procession. A fellowship, a professorship, he felt capable of anything and saw himself – but what was she looking at? At a man pasting a bill. The vast flapping sheet flattened itself out, and each shove of the brush revealed fresh legs, hoops, horses, glistening reds and blues, beautifully smooth, until half the wall was covered with the advertisement of a circus; a hundred horsemen, twenty performing seals, lions, tigers . . . Craning forwards, for she was short-sighted, she read out how it . . . 'will visit this town.' It was terribly dangerous work for a one-armed man, she exclaimed, to stand on top of a ladder like that – his left arm had been cut off in a reaping machine two years go.

'Let us all go!' she cried, moving on, as if all those riders and horses had filled her with child-like exultation and made her forget her pity.

'Let's go,' he said, repeating her words, clicking them out, however, with a self-consciousness that made her wince. 'Let us all go to the Circus.' No. He could not say it right. He could not feel it right. But why not? she wondered. What was wrong with him then? She liked him warmly, at the moment. Had they not been taken, she asked, to circuses when they were children? Never, he answered, as if she asked the very thing he wanted to reply to; had been longing all these days to say, how they did not go to circuses. It was a large family, nine brothers and sisters, and his father was a working man. 'My father is a chemist, Mrs Ramsay. He keeps a shop.' He himself had paid his own way since he was thirteen. Often he went without a greatcoat in winter. He could never 'return hospitality' (those were his parched stiff words) at college. He had to make things last twice the time other people did; he smoked the cheapest tobacco; shag; the same the old men smoked on the quays. He worked hard – seven hours a day; his subject was now the influence of something upon somebody – they were walking on and Mrs Ramsay did not quite catch the meaning, only the words, here and there . . . dissertation . . . fellowship . . . readership . . . lectureship. She could not follow the ugly academic jargon, that rattled itself off so glibly, but said to herself that she saw now why going to the circus had knocked him off his perch, poor little man, and why he came out, instantly, with all that about his father and mother and brothers and sisters, and she would see to it that they didn't laugh at him any more; she would tell Prue about it. What he would have liked, she supposed, would have been to say how he had gone not to the circus but to Ibsen with the Ramsays. He was an awful prig – oh yes, an insufferable bore. For, though they had reached the town now and were in the main street, with carts grinding past on the cobbles, still he went on talking, about settlements, and teaching, and working men, and helping our own class, and lectures, till she gathered that he had got back entire self-confidence, had recovered from the circus, and was about (and now again she liked him warmly) to tell her – but here, the houses falling away on both sides, they came out on the quay, and the whole bay spread before them and Mrs Ramsay could not help exclaiming, 'Oh, how beautiful!' For the great plateful of blue water was before her; the hoary Lighthouse, distant, austere, in the midst; and on the right, as far as the eye could see, fading and falling, in soft low pleats, the green sand dunes with the wild flowing grasses on them, which always seemed to be running away into some moon country, uninhabited by men.

That was the view, she said, stopping, growing greyer-eyed, that her husband loved.

She paused a moment. But now, she said, artists had come here. There indeed, only a few paces off, stood one of them, in Panama hat and yellow boots, seriously, softly, absorbedly, for all that he was watched by ten little boys, with an air of profound contentment on his round red face, gazing, and then, when he gazed, dipping; imbuing the tip of his brush in some soft mound of green or pink. Since Mr Pauncefort had been there, three years before, all the pictures were like that she said, green and grey, with lemon-coloured sailing-boats, and pink women on the beach.

But her grandmother's friends, she said, glancing discreetly as they passed, took the greatest pains; first they mixed their own colours, and then they ground them, and then they put damp cloths on them to keep them moist.

So Mr Tansley supposed she meant him to see that that man's pictures were skimpy, was that what one said? The colours weren't solid? Was that what one said? Under the influence of that extraordinary emotion which had been growing all the walk, had begun in the garden when he had wanted to take her bag, had increased in the town when he had wanted to tell her everything about himself, he was coming to see himself, and everything he had ever known gone crooked a little. It was awfully strange.

There he stood in the parlour of the poky little house where she had taken him, waiting for her, while she went upstairs for a moment to see the woman. He heard her quick step above; heard her voice cheerful, then low; looked at the mats, tea-caddies, glass shades; waited quite impatiently; looked forward eagerly to the walk home, determined to carry her bag; then heard her come out; shut a door; say they must keep the windows open and the doors shut, ask at the house for anything they wanted (she must be talking to a child), when, suddenly, in she came, stood for a moment silent (as if she had been pretending up there, and for a moment let herself be now), stood quite motionless for a moment against a picture of Queen Victoria wearing the blue ribbon of the Garter; and all at once he realised that it was this: – she was the most beautiful person he had ever seen.

With stars in her eyes and veils in her hair, with cyclamen and wild violets – what nonsense was he thinking? She was fifty at least; she had eight children. Stepping through fields of flowers and taking to her breast buds that had broken and lambs that had fallen; with the stars in her eyes and the wind in her hair – He had hold of her bag.

'Good-bye, Elsie,' she said, and they walked up the street, she holding her parasol erect and walking as if she expected to meet someone round the corner, while for the first time in his life Charles Tansley felt an extraordinary pride; a man digging in a drain stopped digging and looked at her; let his arm fall down and looked at her; Charles Tansley felt an extraordinary pride; felt the wind and the cyclamen and the violets for he was walking with a beautiful woman for the first time in his life. He had hold of her bag.

Dorothy L. Sayers, *Have His Carcase* (1932)

Thursday, 18 June

The best remedy for a bruised heart is not, as so many people seem to think, repose upon a manly bosom. Much more efficacious are honest work, physical activity, and the sudden acquisition of wealth. After being acquitted of murdering her lover, and, indeed, in consequence of that acquittal, Harriet Vane found all three specifics abundantly at her disposal; and although Lord Peter Wimsey, with a touching faith in tradition, persisted day in and day out in presenting his bosom for her approval, she showed no inclination to recline upon it.

Work she had in abundance. To be tried for murder is a fairly good advertisement for a writer of detective fiction. Harriet Vane thrillers were booming. She had signed up sensational contracts in both continents, and found herself, consequently, a very much richer woman than she had ever dreamed of becoming. In the interval between finishing *Murder by Degrees* and embarking on *The Fountain-Pen Mystery*, she had started off on a solitary walking-tour: plenty of exercise, no responsibilities, and no letters forwarded. The time was June, the weather perfect; and if she now and again gave a thought to Lord Peter Wimsey diligently ringing up an empty flat, it did not trouble her, or cause her to alter her steady course along the south-west coast of England.

On the morning of the 18th June, she set out from Lesston Hoe with the intention of walking along the cliffs to Wilvercombe, sixteen miles away. Not that she particularly looked forward to Wilvercombe, with its seasonal population of old ladies and invalids and its subdued attempts at the gay life, seeming somehow themselves all a little invalid and old-ladyish. But the town made a convenient objective, and one could always choose some more rural spot for a night's lodging. The coast-road ran pleasantly at the top of a low range of cliffs, from which she could look down upon the yellow stretch of the beach, broken here and there by scattered rocks, which rose successively, glistening in the sunlight, from the reluctant and withdrawing tide.

Overhead, the sky arched up to an immense dome of blue, just fretted here and there with faint white clouds, very high and filmy. The wind blew from the west, very softly, though the weather-wise might have detected in it a tendency to freshen. The road, narrow and in poor repair, was almost deserted, all the heavy traffic passing by the wider arterial road which ran importantly inland from town to town, despising the windings of the coast with its few scattered hamlets. Here and there a drover passed her with his dog, man and beast alike indifferent and preoccupied; here and there a couple of horses out at grass lifted shy and foolish eyes to look after her; here and there a herd of cows, rasping their jawbones upon a stone wall, greeted her with heavy snufflings. From time to time the white sail of a fishing-boat broke the seaward horizon. Except for an occasional tradesman's van or a dilapidated Morris, and the intermittent appearance of white smoke from a distant railway-engine, the landscape was as rural and solitary as it might have been two hundred years before.

Harriet walked sturdily onwards, the light pack upon her shoulders interfering little with her progress. She was twenty-eight years old, dark, slight, with a skin naturally a little sallow, but now tanned to an agreeable biscuit-colour by the sun and wind. Persons of this fortunate complexion are not troubled by midges and sunburn, and Harriet, though not too old to care for her personal appearance, was old enough to prefer convenience to outward display. Consequently, her luggage was not burdened by skin-creams, insect-lotion, silk frocks, portable electric irons, or other impedimenta beloved of the 'Hikers' Column'. She was dressed sensibly in a short skirt and thin sweater, and carried, in addition to a change of linen and an extra provision of footwear, little else beyond a pocket edition of *Tristram Shandy*, a vest-pocket camera, a small first-aid outfit, and a sandwich lunch.

It was about a quarter to one when the matter of the lunch began to loom up importantly in Harriet's mind. She had come about eight miles on her way to Wilvercombe, having taken things easily and made a detour to inspect certain Roman remains declared by the guide-book to be 'of considerable interest'. She began to feel both weary and hungry, and looked about her for a suitable lunching-place.

The tide was nearly out now, and the wet beach shimmered golden and silvery in the lazy noonlight. It would be pleasant, she thought, to go down to the shore – possibly even to bathe, though she did not feel too certain about that, having a wholesome dread of unknown shores and eccentric currents.

Still, there was no harm in going to see. She stepped over the low wall which bounded the road on the seaward side and set about looking for a way down. A short scramble among rocks tufted with scabious and seapink brought her easily down to the beach. She found herself in a small cove, comfortably screened from the wind by an outstanding mass of cliff, and with a few convenient boulders against which to sit. She selected the cosiest spot, drew out her lunch and *Tristram Shandy*, and settled down.

There is no more powerful lure to slumber than hot sunshine on a sea-beach after lunch; nor is the pace of *Tristram Shandy* so swift as to keep the faculties working at high pressure. Harriet found the book escaping her fingers. Twice she caught it back with a jerk; the third time it eluded her altogether. Her head drooped over at an unbecoming angle. She dozed off.

She was awakened suddenly by what seemed to be a shout or cry almost in her ear. As she sat up, blinking, a gull swooped close over her head, squawking and hovering over a stray fragment of sandwich. She shook herself reprovingly and glanced at her wristwatch. It was two o'clock. Realizing with satisfaction that she could not have slept very long, she scrambled to her feet, and shook the crumbs from her lap. Even now she did not feel very energetic, and there was plenty of time to make Wilvercombe before evening. She glanced out to sea, where a long belt of shingle and a narrow strip of virgin and shining sand stretched down to the edge of the water.

There is something about virgin sand which arouses all the worst instincts of the detective-story writer. One feels an irresistible impulse to go and make footprints all over it. The excuse which the professional mind makes to itself is that the sand affords a grand opportunity for observation and experiment. Harriet was no stranger to this impulse. She determined to walk out across that tempting strip of sand. She gathered her various belongings together and started off across the loose shingle, observing, as she had often observed before, that footsteps left no distinguishable traces in the arid region above high-water mark.

Soon, a little belt of broken shells and half-dry seaweed showed that the tide-mark had been reached.

'I wonder,' said Harriet to herself, 'whether I ought to be able to deduce something or other about the state of the tides. Let me see. When the tide is at neaps, it doesn't rise or fall so far as when it is at springs. Therefore, if that is the case, there ought to be two seaweedy marks – one quite dry and further in, showing the highest point of spring tides, and one damper and further down, showing today's best effort.' She glanced backwards and forwards. 'No; this is the only tide-mark. I deduce, therefore, that I have arrived somewhere about the top of springs, if that's the proper phrase. Perfectly simple, my dear Watson. Below tide-mark, I begin to make definite footprints. There are no others anywhere, so that I must be the only person who has patronized this beach since last high tide, which would be about – ah! yes, there's the difficulty. I know there should be about twelve hours between one tide and the next, but I haven't the foggiest notion whether the sea is coming in or going out. Still, I do know it was going out most of the time as I came along, and it looks a long way off now. If I say that nobody has been here for the last five hours I shan't be far out. I'm making very pretty footprints now, and the sand is, naturally, getting wetter. I'll see how it looks when I run.'

She capered a few paces accordingly, noticing the greater depth of the toe-prints and the little spurt of sand thrown out at each step. This outburst of energy brought her round the point of the cliff and into a much larger bay, the only striking feature of which was a good-sized rock, standing down at the sea's edge, on the other side of the point. It was roughly triangular in shape, standing about ten feet out of the water, and seemed to be crowned with a curious lump of black seaweed.

A solitary rock is always attractive. All right-minded people feel an overwhelming desire to scale and sit upon it. Harriet made for it without any mental argument, trying to draw a few deductions as she went.

'Is that rock covered at high tide? Yes, of course, or it wouldn't have seaweed on top. Besides, the slope of the shore proves it. I wish I was better at distances and angles, but I should say it would be covered pretty deep. How odd that it should have seaweed only in that lump at the top. You'd expect it at the foot, but the sides seem quite bare, nearly down to the water. I suppose it *is* seaweed. It's very peculiar. It looks almost more like a man lying down; is it possible for seaweed to be so very – well, so very localized?'

She gazed at the rock with a faint stirring of curiosity, and went on talking aloud to herself, as was her rather irritating habit.

'I'm dashed if it isn't a man lying down. What a silly place to choose. He must feel like a bannock on a hot griddle. I could understand if he was a sun-bathing fan, but he seems to have got all his clothes on. A dark suit at that. He's very quiet. He's probably fallen asleep. If the tide comes in at all fast, he'll be cut off, like the people in the silly magazine stories. Well, I'm not going to rescue him. He'll have to take his socks off and paddle, that's all. There's plenty of time yet.'

She hesitated whether to go on down the rock. She did not want to wake the sleeper and be beguiled into conversation. Not but what he would prove to be some perfectly harmless tripper. But he would certainly be somebody quite uninteresting. She went on, however, meditating, and drawing a few more deductions by way of practice.

'He must be a tripper. Local inhabitants don't take their siestas on rocks. They retire indoors and shut all the windows. And he can't be a fisherman or anything of that kind; they don't waste time snoozing. Only the black-coated brigade does that. Let's call him a tradesman or a bank clerk. But then they usually take their holidays complete with family. This is a solitary sort of fowl. A schoolmaster? No. Schoolmasters don't get off the lead till the end of July. How about a college undergraduate? It's only *just* the end of term. A gentleman of no particular occupation, apparently. Possibly a walking tourist like myself – but the costume doesn't look right.' She had come nearer now and could see the sleeper's dark suit quite plainly. 'Well I can't place him, but no doubt Dr Thorndyke would do so at once. Oh, of course. How stupid! He must be a literary bloke of some kind. They moon about and don't let their families bother them.'

She was within a few yards of the rock now, gazing up at the sleeper. He lay uncomfortably bunched-up on the extreme seaward edge of the rock, his knees drawn high and showing his pale mauve socks. The head, tucked closely down between the shoulders, was invisible.

'What a way to sleep,' said Harriet. 'More like a cat than a human being. It's not natural. His head must be almost hanging over the edge. It's enough to give him apoplexy. Now, if I had any luck, he'd be a corpse, and I should report him and get my name in the papers. That would be something like publicity. "Well-known Woman Detective-Writer Finds Mystery Corpse on Lonely Shore." But these things never happen to authors. It's always some placid labourer or night-watchman who finds corpses . . .'

The rock lay tilted like a gigantic wedge of cake, its base standing steeply up to seaward, its surface sloping gently back to where its apex entered the sand. Harriet climbed up over its smooth, dry surface till she stood almost directly over the man. He did not move at all. Something impelled her to address him.

'Oy!' she said, protestingly.

There was neither movement nor reply.

'I'd just as soon he didn't wake up,' thought Harriet. 'I can't imagine what I'm shouting for. *Oy!*'

'Perhaps he's in a fit or a faint,' she said to herself. 'Or he's got sunstroke. That's quite likely. It's very hot.' She looked up, blinking, at the brazen sky, then stooped and laid one hand on the surface of the rock. It almost burnt her. She shouted again, and then, bending over the man, seized his shoulder.

'Are you all right?'

The man said nothing and she pulled upon the shoulder. It shifted slightly – a dead weight. She bent over and gently lifted the man's head.

Harriet's luck was in.

It *was* a corpse. Not the sort of corpse there could be any doubt about, either. Mr Samuel Weare of Lyons Inn, whose 'throat they cut from ear to ear', could not have been more indubitably a corpse. Indeed, if the head did not come off in Harriet's hands, it was only because the spine was intact, for the larynx and all the great vessels of the neck had been severed 'to the hause-bone', and a frightful stream, bright red and glistening, was running over the surface of the rock and dripping into a little hollow below.

Harriet put the head down again and felt suddenly sick. She had written often enough about this kind of corpse, but meeting the thing in the flesh was quite different. She had not realized how butcherly the severed vessels would look, and she had not reckoned with the horrid halitus of blood, which steamed to her nostrils under the blazing sun. Her hands were red and wet. She looked down at her dress. That had escaped, thank goodness. Mechanically she stepped down again from the rock and went round to the edge of the sea. There she washed her fingers over and over again, drying them with ridiculous care upon her handkerchief. She did not like the look of the red trickle that dripped down the face of the rock into the clear water. Retreating, she sat down rather hastily on some loose boulders.

'A dead body,' said Harriet, aloud to the sun and the seagulls. 'A dead body. How – how appropriate!' She laughed.

Nan Shepherd, 'Summit of Coire Etchachan', from *In the Cairngorms* (1934)

But in the climbing ecstasy of thought,
Ere consummation, ere the final peak,
Come hours like this. Behind, the long defile,
The steep rock-path, alongside which, from under
Snow-caves, sharp-corniced, tumble the ice-cold waters,
And now, here, at the corrie's summit, no peak,
No vision of the blue world, far, unattainable,
But this grey plateau, rock-strewn, vast, silent,
The dark loch, the toiling crags, the snow;
A mountain shut within itself, yet a world,
Immensity. So may the mind achieve,
Toiling, no vision of the infinite,
But a vast, dark and inscrutable sense
Of its own terror, its own glory and power.

Virginia Woolf, *The Diary of Virginia Woolf*, Tuesday, 2 October 1934

Yes, but my head will never let me glory sweepingly: always a tumble. Yesterday morning the old rays of light set in; & then the sharp, the very sharp pain over my eyes; so that I sat & lay about till tea; had no walk, had not a single idea of triumph or relief. L. bought me a little travelling ink pot, by way of congratulation. I wish I could think of a name. Sons & Daughters? Probably used already. Theres a mass to be done to the last chapter, which I shall, I hope, dv. as they say in some circles, I suppose still, begin tomorrow: while the putty is still soft.

So the summer is ended. Until the 9th of Sept: when Nessa came across the terrace – how I hear that cry Hes dead – a very vigorous, happy summer. Oh the joy of walking! I've never felt it so strong in me. Cowper Powys, oddly enough, expresses the same thing: the trance like, swimming, flying through the air; the current of sensations & ideas; & the slow, but fresh change of down, of road, of colour: all this churned up into a fine thin sheet of perfect calm happiness. Its true I often painted the brightest pictures on this sheet: & often talked aloud. Lord how many pages of Sons & Daughters – perhaps Daughters & Sons would give a rhythm more unlike

Sons & Lovers, or Wives & Daughters [*by Mrs Gaskell*], –
I made up, chattering them in my excitement on the top of
the down, in the folds.

Frieda Lawrence, *Not I, But the Wind . . .* (1935)

It was in the middle of August that we set out gaily. Neither of us knew Italy at the time, it was a great adventure for both. We packed up our few possessions, three trunks went ahead of us to the Lago di Garda. We set off on foot, with a rucksack each and a Burberry. In the rucksack was a little spirit lamp, we were going to cook our food by the roadside for cheapness.

We started on a misty morning very thrilled. The trees were dripping along the road, but we were happy in our adventure, free, going to unknown parts. We walked along the solid green of the valley of the Isar, we climbed up hills and went down again. One of my desires, to sleep in haylofts, was fulfilled. But sleeping in haylofts is uncomfortable, really. It rained so much and we were soaked. And the wind blows through haylofts and if you cover yourself with a ton of hay you still can't get warm . . .

Lawrence's birthday came as we were crossing the Alps. I had no present to give him but some edelweiss. That evening we danced and drank beer with the peasants in the Gasthaus of the village we were passing through. His first birthday together. It was all very wonderful. New things happened all the time . . .

How I want to recapture the gaiety of that adventurous walk into Italy, romantic Italy, with all its glamour and sunshine.

We arrived at Trento, but alas for the glamour! We could only afford a very cheap hotel and the marks on the walls, the doubtful sheets, and worst of all the w.c.s were too much for me.

The people were strangers, I could not speak Italian, then.

So, one morning, much to Lawrence's dismay, he found me sitting on a bench under the statue of Dante, weeping bitterly. He had seen me walk barefoot over icy stubble, laughing at wet and hunger and cold; it had all seemed only fun to me, and here I was crying because of the city-uncleanness and the w.c.s. It had taken us about six weeks to get there.

Sylvia Townsend Warner, *Summer Will Show* (1936)

Later in the evening she had good bodily reason to remember the Lithuanian childhood, the free wanderings over the heath. Minna still walked as though her foot were on a heath, and as though conducting her from one bird's-nest to another she led Sophia by innumerable short-cuts to various places where the Revolution might be expected to make a good showing. At least a dozen barricades were visited, and over these they had been handed with great civility; falling in with a procession they followed it to the Place de la Bastille, where they waited for some time, listening to the singing, and then in the wake of another procession they had trudged to the Hôtel de Ville and listened to shouting. The shouting was all, presumably, that revolutionary shouting should be – loud, confident, and affable. Here and there, bursting upwards from the level of the crowd, an orator would emerge, twine like some short-lived flower to railings, and sum up in a more polished and blossom-like fashion the sentiments of the shouters.

But shaking her head in critical dissatisfaction, Minna said, 'There is more to see than this.'

'Shall we try the Champs-Élysées?' For there at any rate, thought Sophia, there will be a chance to sit down. She was intolerably footsore, and in the reality of that sensation could feel nothing but despising for a revolution that was no concern of hers.

'No.'

Minna turned northward again. As they went farther it began to seem as though they were the only people walking that way. Here there was little uproar, no illuminations, no processions – but like leaves blown on some steady wind a man, or three men, or six men, would come towards them and pass them. They spoke very little, their faces wore no particular expression except the look of wariness which comes on the faces of all those who have to strive for a living. They seemed in no great hurry, tramping on as though they were going to their work. Among them, moving more swiftly as though they were lighter leaves on the same steady wind, came coveys of children, and groups of women, marching abreast with linked arms. And while their following shadows still trailed on the pavement, on into the circle of lamplight would come one man, three men, six men.

'Do you see,' whispered Minna. 'It is the same yet, the old nursery of revolutions.'

'It frightens me,' said Sophia. 'And I believe that you, even, are a little afraid.'

'A little? I am horribly afraid. How is it possible to have a good bed to sleep in, food in the larder, furs against the cold, books on one's shelves, money in one's purse, a taste for music, and not be afraid? It is ten years and more, thanks to my good fortune, since I could have looked at these without being afraid.'

'But you believe in revolution?'

'With all my heart.'

They turned back, walking on the same wind as those others. Sophia began to make conversation about Socialism, endeavouring to blame it as coolly as possible, pointing out that equality was a delusion, that the poor in office were the cruellest oppressors of the poor, etc. By the time they struck the boulevard des Capucines the changed character of the crowd had restored to her enough confidence to let the conversation drop. For here they were back once more in the heartiest display of comic opera. Earlier in the day the property rooms of the theatres had been raided by some enterprising collectors of arms, and under the light of the illuminations gilded spears and pasteboard helmets still wreathed with artificial flowers mingled their classical elegance with the morions and pikes which had last appeared in performances of *I Puritani*. Moving slowly through the crowd were family groups of sight-seers, who had come out to enjoy the illuminations.

'That's nice, that one,' said a woman behind Sophia, pointing to a housefront garlanded with little coloured lamps, hanging on wires like festoons of fruit and centring in a large and miscellaneous trophy of flags.

'They should include the ground-floor,' her companion answered with a laugh of superior sarcasm; and looking more attentively, Sophia saw that the ground-floor windows had been boarded up, and that a detachment of soldiers was on guard before the house.

Cheerfully, politely, as though the information would make amends for the partial embellishment only, the woman exclaimed,

'Look, Anatole! Another procession, and this one with torches!'

'They've been quadrilling outside the *National*,' replied the well-informed Anatole. 'Old Marrast has been letting off another of his speeches to them.'

'Children too. The little darlings, how pleased they look! I hope they won't set fire to anything with those torches. I'm glad now that we left Louise and Albertine at home. They would never be content until – '

The surging of the crowd carried them away from the words. Sophia tightened her hold on Minna's elbow, and stiffened herself protectively. Weary, footsore, sleepy, and bored, she still retained a core of carefulness for her companion, the last ember of emotion left waking from the earlier day.

Nan Shepherd to Neil Gunn, 14 May 1940

Laddie, you frighten me whiles. Not because of the theme, or any consideration of its implications: but because of the uncanny way you enter my breathing and living and seeing and apprehending. To apprehend things – walking on a hill, seeing the light change, the mist, the dark, being aware, using the whole of one's body to instruct the spirit – yes, that is a secret life one has and knows that others have. But to be able to share it, in and through words – that's what frightens me. The word shouldn't have such power. It dissolves one's being. I am no longer myself but part of a life beyond myself when I read pages that are so much the expression of myself. You can take processes of being – no, that's too formal a words – states is too static, this is something that moves – movements I suppose is best – you can take movements of being and translate them out of themselves into words. That seems to me a gift of a very high and rare order.

Anaïs Nin, 'The Labyrinth', from *Under a Glass Bell* (1944)

I was eleven years old when I walked into the labyrinth of my diary. I carried it in a little basket and climbed the moldy steps of a Spanish garden and came upon boxed streets in neat order in a backyard of a house in New York, I walked protected by dark green shadows and followed a design I was sure to remember. I wanted to remember in order to be able to return. As I walked, I walked with the desire to see all things twice so as to find my way back into them again. The bushes were soft hairy elbows touching mine, the branches swords over my head. They led me. I did not count the turns, the chess moves, the mediated displacements, the obsessional repetitions. The repetitions prevented me from counting the hours and the steps. The obsessions became the infinite. I was lost. I only stopped because of the clock pointing to anguish. An anguish about returning and about seeing these things but once. There was a definite feeling that their meaning could only be revealed the second time. If I were forced to go on, unknowing, blind, everything would be lost. I was infinitely far from my first steps. I did not know exactly why I must return. I did not know that at the end I would not find myself where I started. The beginning and the end were different, and why should the coming to an end annihilate the beginning? And why should the beginning be retained? I did not know, but for the anguish in my being, an anguish over something lost. The darkness before me was darker than the darkness behind me.

Everything was so much the same and equal before and around me that I was not certain I had turned sufficiently in the path to be actually walking towards the place from which I started. The clouds were the same, the croaking of the frogs, the soft rain sound of fountains, and the immobile green flame of evergreens in boxes. I was walking on a carpet of pages without number. Why had I not numbered the pages? Because I was aware of what I had left out; so much was left out that I had intended to insert, and numbering was impossible, for numbering would mean I had said everything. I was walking up a stairway of words. The words repeated themselves. I was walking on the word pity pity pity pity pity pity pity. My step covered the whole word each time, but then I saw I was not walking. When the word was the same, it did not move, nor did my feet. The word died. And the anguish came, about the death of this word, about the death of the feeling inside of this word. The landscape did not change, the walk was without corners; the paths so mysteriously enchained I never knew when I had turned to the right or left. I was walking on the word obsession with naked feet: the trees seemed to press closer together, and breathing was difficult. I was seeking the month, the year, the hour, which might have helped me to return. In front of me was a tunnel of darkness which sucked me violently ahead, while the anguish pulled me backwards. The escalator of words ran swiftly under me, like a river. I was walking on my rebellions, stones exploding under my feet.

Following the direction of their heaviest fragment might take me back. Yet all the time I knew that what I would find would be white bleached bones, sand, ashes, decomposed smiles, eyes full of holes like cooled lava.

My feet were slipping on accumulated tears like the slippery silt of river banks, on stones washed by slow waters. I touched rock-crystal walls with white foaming crevices, white sponges of secret sorrows set in a lace of plant skeletons. Leaves, skins, flesh had been sucked of their juices and the juices and sap drunk by the crevices, flowing together through the river bed of stillborn desires.

Legs and arms and ears of wax were hung as offerings, yielded to the appetite of the cave, nailed with humble prayers for protection that the demon might not devour those who passed.

I walked pinned to a spider web of fantasies spun during the night, obstinately followed during the day. This spider web was broken by a foghorn, and by the chiming of the hours. I found myself traversing gangways, moats, gangplanks while still tied to the heaving straining cord of a departing ship. I was suspended between earth and sea, between earth and planets. Traversing them in haste, with anguish for the shadow left behind, the foot's imprint, the echo. All cords easily untied but the one binding me to what I loved.

I sank into a labyrinth of silence. My feet were covered with fur, my hand with leather, my legs wrapped in accordian-pleated cotton, tied with silken whips. Reindeer fur on my breast. Voicelessness. I knew that like the reindeer even if the knife were thrust into me at this moment, I would not even sigh.

Fragments of the dream exploded during my passage through the moats, fell like cutting pieces from dead planets without cutting through the fur and cotton of this silence. The flesh and fur walls breathed and drops of white blood fell with the sound of a heartbeat. I did not want to advance into the silence, feeling I might lose my voice forever. I moved my lips to remember the words I had formed, but I felt they no longer articulated words. My lips moved like the sea anemone, with infinite slowness, opening and closing, rolling under the exterior pressure, to breathe, forming nothing but a design in water. Or they moved like the noses of animals quivering at the passing wind, to detect, to feel, forming no word but recognition of an odor. Or they moved as flowers close for the night, or against the invasion of an insect. They breathed with fine slowness, with the cadence of a bulb flowering.

I was not moving any more with my feet. The cave was no longer an endless route opening before me. It was a wooden, fur-lined crib, swinging. When I ceased stepping firmly, counting my steps, when I ceased feeling the walls around me with fingers twisted like roots, seeking nourishment, the labyrinthian walk became enlarged, the silence became airy, the fur disintegrated, and I walked into a white city.

It was a honeycomb of ivory-white cells, streets like ribbons of old ermine. The stone and mortar were mixed with sunlight, with musk and white cotton. I passed by streets of peace lying entangled like cotton spools, serpentines of walls without doorways, veiled faces and veiled windows ascending, dissolving into terraces, courtyards, emptying into the river. I heard secret fountains of laughter, hooded voices. I heard the evening prayer like a lament spilling on shining mosaics and

the veins of the cobblestones under my feet were like a chaplet
between monks' fingers. I passed windowless houses erupting
at the tip in flowered terraces, a Vesuvius of flowers. And now
I was inside the soft turning canals of a giant ear, inside the
leaves of intricate flowers, streets spiralling like sea shells, lost
in a point, and the bodies passing me were wrapped in cotton
capes, and breathed into each other's faces. In their hands the
sand of time was passing slowly. They carried enormous rusty
keys to open the gates which divided the city. The palm leaves
were waving, gently content, and the city lay like a carpet
under contemplative feet. I was awakened by a sound of paper
unrolling. My feet were treading paper. They were the streets
of my own diary, crossed with bars of black notes. Serpentines
of walls without doorways, desires without issues. I was lost
in the labyrinth of my confessions, among the veiled faces of
my acts unveiled only in the diary. I heard the evening prayer,
the cry of solitude recurring every night. My feet touched the
leaves of intricate flowers shrivelling, paper flowers veined with
the nerves of instruments. Enormous rusty keys opened each
volume, and the figures passed armless, headless, mutilated.
The white orifice of the endless cave opened. On the rim of it
stood a girl eleven years old carrying the diary in a little basket.

Flora Thompson, *Heatherley* (1944)

Her work at the post office, making new friends and reading new library books in quick succession, did not fill the whole of Laura's life at this time. She had another interest which, though she was able to devote less time to it, lay nearer her heart's core.

Her love of nature was an inborn love and she was quick to recognize natural beauty even in those places where such beauty was not spectacular. In her own county, where the landscape as a whole was plain and homely, there were many sweet scenes which were dear to her. Buttercup meadows set round with dark elms, deep double hedgerows white with may, festooned with wild rose or honeysuckle, or berried with hips and haws and hung with big silvery puffs of old-man's beard, according to season. And there were little brooks, banked with willow herb and meadowsweet, which meandered through fields where in spring skylarks soared and sang above the young green wheat, or patches of bright yellow mustard; and later in the year when the small birds were silent and coveys of young partridge chicks scurried *peep-peeping* to cover before an approaching footstep on the field paths, those same fields would be golden with ripe grain and there would be poppies in the corn.

And since she had left home, although she had not actually seen the sea, she had seen an Essex saltmarsh bluish-mauve with sea lavender, and a tidal river with red fisher sails upon it and gulls wheeling overhead and seaweed clinging to the stones of its quays. All those things she had loved and would always love. If she had been condemned to live in a great city for the rest of her life they would still have been hers, for nothing could rob her of such memories.

Her love of her own country was that of a child for its parent, a love which takes all for granted, instinctive rather than inspiring, but lifelong. Her love of the Heatherley countryside was of a different nature. It had come to her suddenly in that moment of revelation when, on the day of her arrival, she had unexpectedly come out on the heath and seen the heather in bloom. She had felt then a quick, conscious sense of being one with her surroundings, and as she came to know the hills and heaths in all moods and seasons, the feeling became more definite. It was more a falling in love on her part than of merely loving.

After she had become established at Heatherley her greatest pleasure in life was in her few free daylight hours to roam on the heather-clad hills or to linger in one of the valley woods where trickling watercourses fed the lush greenery of ferns and bracken and mosses and the very light which filtered down through the low, matted overgrowth was tinged with green. She liked best to walk in those places alone, for although she soon made a few friends, a walk in their company, she found, meant a brisk swinging progress from point to point to the accompaniment of much talk and laughter. Such walks could be taken on dark evenings after the office was closed and they were then often taken by Laura with great enjoyment. But she loved best her solitary walks, when she could stand and gaze at some favourite viewpoint, watch the heath birds and insects and quick-darting lizards, gather the heath flowers into little stiff honey-scented bouquets, run the warm, clean heath sands through her fingers and bare her head to the soft, misty rain.

Sunday morning, after the office had closed, was the best time, and in winter the only time for these solitary walks. With good luck in the matter of work, she would have her hat and coat already on when the telegraph instrument ticked out its daily message from Greenwich: 'T-*i-m-e* – T-*i-m-e* – T-*i-m-e*', then, after a few seconds' pause, 'T-E-N!' A moment later she would have locked the door behind her and be halfway down the village street on her way to the hills or woods. During the Boer War, with wireless broadcasts far in the future and only very early editions, printed the day before, of the Sunday newspapers reaching many places, the Government authorities thought it necessary to institute Sunday morning bulletins giving the latest war news. These were telegraphed to every post office to be written out and displayed in the post-office windows. The bulletin was supposed to arrive before ten o'clock, when the offices closed. Occasionally it did arrive before ten, but far more often, at Heatherley, it came a quarter, a half, or sometimes a whole hour after that time. Laura, who had no objection on other days to staying beyond her hours to complete this or that, found this involuntary Sunday overtime exasperating, for it shortened her walk.

When, sooner or later, she was at liberty, it took her but a few minutes to reach open country. Looking neither to right nor left lest she should see some acquaintance who would volunteer to come with her, she would rush like a bandersnatch, as someone once said who had seen her from a distance, and take the first turning out of the village which led to the heath.

Jessie Kesson, 'Blaeberry Wood' (1945)

Our Street had a face I did not know, in the early
   morning light –
Not tired and hot and crowded, as it had looked
   last night.
I came upon it unawares,
Before the day, with pressing cares,
And noise and dust and weary heat,
Unceasing tramp of hurrying feet,
Had caught it up. Night must have lent some magic
   to Our Street.
And deep in me arose an eagerness
That I must dance to show my happiness.
But there was never an eye to see
This fun and gaiety of me.
Yet I knew someone understood.
'Twas all because of Blaeberry Wood.
Down our Close, up Murdoch's Wynd,
I left the East-end far behind,
And now must walk with quiet feet
Along West Road – the rich folks' Street,
With villas standing stiff and prim,

Each with its garden neat and trim.
They all seemed very much the same
But for a number or a name.
And yet their dust-bins in a row
Made my heart beat, my eyes to glow.
How carefully I'd search each bin,
Excited, plunging headlong in
For a broken doll or a coloured tin.
Sometimes a dog would come as well,
And prowl around, and smell and smell.
Wagging his tail, to the next he'd run,
As if he, too, found dust-bins fun.
Life at the child must often smile –
The rich folks' dust-bins a Treasure Isle!
And now the long straight country road
With my dust-bin booty for my load.
Here was the wood. Within I flew
To a secret spot that alone I knew,
Where hyacinths, wild and wet and blue
In their hundreds and hundreds grew.
There on the wet grass, on my knees,
I pressed my face in the heart of these.
No smell I know is half so good
As the hyacinth tang in a morning wood.
I ever saw them with new eyes.
My heart was quick to meet surprise.
So now I set to work with a will.
'I think my pail will never fill.'
The rustling trees and the rising wind;
The town's left ever so far behind.

And the crackling twigs, and the bird-calls shrill;
The wood was never a moment still.
And now the droning of a bee.
Everything's busy round here – but me.
I just watch and watch the hole by the tree
For the rabbit that I was never to see.
The sun grows warm. The moss is deep.
I'd like to sink – and to sleep and sleep.
It's colder now. I think I'll call;
The world is strange when the shadows fall.
I'm not afraid, afraid at all;
But, all the same, I think I'll call.
Now where's my doll and flowers and tin?
What can I carry the whole of them in?
If I but could, if I but could,
I'd have carried away the half of the wood
Home in my arms. The foxgloves broken,
The hyacinths limp, are just a token.
Every bit of me is blue.
Hands, face, and knees, too.
But my heart has a vivid colour I know.
It's so warm inside me – a fire aglow.
So-long! So-long! It's been a treat.
On my way home again with hurrying feet,
Half-glad, half-sad, back to Our Street.
I'll never grow too old to love Surprise,
Thank God! I still can see through a bairn's eyes.
A bygone trip, an enchanted wood –
A little girl who understood.

Jessie Kesson, 'To Nan Shepherd' (1945)

Two hoors did haud oor years o'kennin' each
    the t'ither's sel',
While words poored forth, swift burns in spate,
syne tint themsel's in the myrrh's thick smell,
We twa grew quate tae listen till oor thochts
gang loupin' through the wuds, and owre
    the distant hills.
Jist aince we cried them back, and changed them
    wi' each ither, like tokens,
Sayin', 'Keep mind o' that still river faur trees glower
    lang an' deep at their reflections'.
Nor could the jostlin' fowk and noisy street touch
    for a meenit oor communion.
Tho' I held oot a hand in pairtin',
I wisna aince my lane on the homeward track.
For, through myrrh's smell, past wud's tremendous
    green,
My frien' just followed me, the hale wye back.

Flora Thompson, *Lark Rise to Candleford* (1945)

School

School began at nine o'clock, but the hamlet children set out on their mile-and-a-half walk there as soon as possible after their seven o'clock breakfast, partly because they liked plenty of time to play on the road and partly because their mothers wanted them out of the way before house-cleaning began.

Up the long, straight road they straggled, in twos and threes and in gangs, their flat, rush dinner-baskets over their shoulders and their shabby little coats on their arms against rain. In cold weather some of them carried two hot potatoes which had been in the oven, or in the ashes, all night, to warm their hands on the way and to serve as a light lunch on arrival.

They were strong, lusty children, let loose from control, and there was plenty of shouting, quarrelling, and often fighting among them. In more peaceful moments they would squat in the dust of the road and play marbles, or sit on a stone heap and play dibs with pebbles, or climb into the hedges after birds' nests or blackberries, or to pull long trails of bryony to wreathe round their hats. In winter they would slide on the ice on the puddles, or make snowballs – soft ones for their friends, and hard ones with a stone inside for their enemies.

After the first mile or so the dinner-baskets would be raided; or they would creep through the bars of the padlocked field gates for turnips to pare with their teeth and munch, or for handfuls of green pea shucks, or ears of wheat, to rub out the sweet, milky grain between the hands and devour. In spring they ate the young green from the hawthorn hedges, which they called 'bread and cheese', and sorrel leaves from the wayside, which they called 'sour grass', and in autumn there was an abundance of haws and blackberries and sloes and crab-apples for them to feast upon. There was always something to eat, and they ate, not so much because they were hungry as from habit and relish of the wild food.

At that early hour there was little traffic upon the road. Sometimes, in winter, the children would hear the pounding of galloping hoofs and a string of hunters, blanketed up to the ears and ridden and led by grooms, would loom up out of the mist and thunder past on the grass verges. At other times the steady tramp and jingle of the teams going afield would approach, and, as they passed, fathers would pretend to flick their offspring with whips, saying. 'There! that's for that time you deserved it an' didn't get it'; while elder brothers, themselves at school only a few months before, would look patronizingly down from the horses' backs and call: 'Get out o' th' way, you kids!'

Going home in the afternoon there was more to be seen. A farmer's gig, on the way home from market, would stir up the dust; or the miller's van or the brewer's dray, drawn by four immense, hairy-legged, satin-backed carthorses. More exciting was the rare sight of Squire Harrison's four-in-hand, with ladies in bright, summer dresses, like a garden of flowers, on the top of the coach, and Squire himself, pink-cheeked and white-hatted, handling the four greys. When the four-in-hand passed, the children drew back and saluted, the Squire would gravely touch the brim of his hat with his whip, and the ladies would lean from their high seats to smile on the curtseying children.

A more familiar sight was the lady on a white horse who rode slowly on the same grass verge in the same direction every Monday and Thursday. It was whispered among the children that she was engaged to a farmer living at a distance, and that they met half-way between their two homes. If so, it must have been a long engagement, for she rode past at exactly the same hour twice a week throughout Laura's schooldays, her face getting whiter and her figure getting fuller and her old white horse also putting on weight.

It has been said that every child is born a little savage and has to be civilized. The process of civilization had not gone very far with some of the hamlet children; although one civilization had them in hand at home and another at school, they were able to throw off both on the road between two places and revert to a state of Nature.

Janet Adam Smith, *Mountain Holidays*
(1946)

This day, to put off the moment of seeing it face to face, I chose to climb first the easy Canisp, which blocks the view; then, grasping the summit cairn firmly, I turned to look at Suilven across the gash of Glen Dorcha. A monster indeed, but at the moment passive. I started up its gentle slopes at the south-east end in sun; but once embarked on the long ridge, down came the mist. Suilven is made up of three humped masses connected by very narrow *bealachs*; as I came over the top of Meall Bheag, the first hump, I could dimly see the slopes of Meall Meadhonach, the second, but I could not see down to the *bealach* in between; when I had groped my way down I found that it consisted of one rock, across which you could straddle – a nice place, and by some freak of wind the mist cleared to the south-west as I sat there a minute, and though I could not see the top I had left five minutes ago, I could see the hills of Skye forty miles away. One the second and broader *bealach*, connecting Meall Meadhonach with Caisteal Liath, the highest, I met a party of three coming back from the top, and realized from their sad and dripping mackintoshes just how wet I must be myself. An easy forty minutes took me to the top of Caisteal Liath – the Grey Castle that faces the

sea, more majestic and less terrifying than the monster seen
from Canisp or the spike from the road to Lairg. But I could
not see the sea, or Lochinver, or the little lochans starring the
moor all round the base of Suilven; and I was beginning to
tire of walking along the wet spine of the monster enclosed in
mist. How dull it would be, I told myself, to retrace my steps
to the *bealach* where I had met the other party, and take the
usual route down the gully. When my other voice remarked
that the dull thing was the only sensible thing on a day like
this, I dismissed it as the devil's guile. Quite wrongly; the
devil in fact was busy at my elbow as I peered over the edge
of the castle ramparts, pointing out to me that there was green
nearly all the way down, and suggesting that I should save time
and energy by descending straight to the string of lochans on
Suilven's northern base.

Gaily I started down. In a quarter of an hour I realized
three things. First, that this north face of the Grey Castle is
made up of continuous rock bands, ten to fifteen feet high,
with grassy terraces between (from above, of course, only the
terraces are visible); second, that these terraces slope outwards;
third, that it would be difficult and lengthy to retrace my
steps because I had zigzagged down a good deal, finding the
weak place in each rock band. Although I knew now which
voice had been the devil's, this last consideration made me
decide to go on, scrambling somehow down the rock band,
then prowling along the grass terrace to find the best place to
attack the next band. This worked all right for a dozen rounds
or so; then came an unfairly high band, perhaps twenty feet,
with no visible cracks, and wet tufts of grass the only apparent
holds. I scouted along the terrace, and finally saw a small ledge

about seven feet down, and a possible foothold about six feet lower. I swung cautiously onto the ledge, did a complicated doubling-up to shoot my feet down to the hold – it was wet and slimy; I had to make up my mind quickly, and I did so by praying hard and jumping for the grass terrace below. I landed square, and everything would have been perfectly all right but for my rucksack, which I had entirely forgotten, and which now swung outwards and twitched me down over the next band. It was a moderate one, only about twelve feet, and the terrace below was flatter than most. So I stopped after one bound, and for two minutes sat and laughed in a loud and silly way at my extremely humiliating but funny situation. 'Here is one calling herself a mountaineer', I mocked, 'fancying her judgement, her eye for a good route, her caution on rock, reduced to falling off a mountain to get down it.' My stockings were ripped, my legs bloody, and my body all bumps, but there seemed to be nothing really wrong as I picked my way as soberly as possible down the rest of the castle wall. Down in the heather I ate an orange, and looked back in clearing weather at Caisteal Liath. From below, of course, the grassy terraces were invisible and the rock bands looked like an uninterrupted face. As I plodded over the weary boggy moorland to reach the road at Little Assynt, I felt I had been let off lightly by the monster.

C. C. Vyvyan, *Down the Rhone on Foot* (1955)

I wanted to stride away while I was able to stride; to embrace the beauty of this universe, my country; to go far away from the hurt that intimate people can inflict, to go where there would be no intimates, only valleys and mountains and strangers, objects separate from oneself as any rock or stone. I wanted to slip out each morning, alone in spirit, far from a reminder of all unhappy days, into a world where dew hung poised on each blade of grass and all seen objects were keeping faith with one another, where bird-song and river-music was welcoming each dawn as a new, unlooked-for benediction. I wanted the companionship of the great self-sufficient river that rushes down its long chasm in Swiss mountains, that achieves peace for a while as it passes through the Lake of Geneva, that winds in loops and gorges westward to Lyon and then moves steadily southward to lose itself, after that long, single-minded journey, in the Mediterranean.

Sometimes in a flash of insight the strangeness of the everyday existence that I should be leading in this adventure would come home to me. With personal possessions reduced, for three whole months, to the contents of a rucksack; with communications cut and friends out of reach; wandering among strange faces every day and speaking a strange language every hour; having no regular occupation save walking, eating and sleeping. I would feel, as I pictured all this, like a rider setting his horse at a fence with his heart in his boots, or an author posting a new M.S., or an orator standing erect just before his words split the silence. The fever of pre-enterprise would have me in its grip.

In other moods, just because I had talked so much about it, the journey would seem straightforward and ordinary. Yet all the time I knew, in that innermost part of being where truth is silently apprehended, that this journey would lead me not only into a world of new roads and faces but also into a new life where I would be 'voyaging in strange seas of thought alone.'

Eleanor Farjeon, *Walking with Edward Thomas: The Last Four Years* (1958)

To walk with Edward Thomas in any countryside was to see, hear, smell and know it with fresh senses. He was as alert to what was happening in and on the earth and the air above it as is an animal in the grass or a bird on a tree. Just as certain friends who share their thoughts with you will sharpen your thinking, he had the effect, when you took the road together, of quickening your seeing and hearing through his own keen eyes and ears. You would not walk that road again as you did before. You would know it in a new way.

He himself was difficult to know. He was a man of moods, and whether he was happy or melancholy he withheld himself. While he shared with you his knowledge of the things that meant most to him, his self-knowledge was what he did not share. He reserved this as a deep pool hides a secret under the surface that reflects clearly every image and movement passing over it. To go for a walk with Edward Thomas was a sure way of discovering something you hadn't noticed about a tree, a weed, a flower, some difference in the sweet or acid notes in birds, how dry earth smells in spring, crumbles darkly in autumn, its freckled look under thaw, the feel of the sun on a stone or on your skin, the weather's changes of mood all the year round. It was also a way of discovering for yourself a little more of the man whose changes of humour resembled the weather, while he was talking of what he deeply loved. He loved equally all things natural, the acid sound and the sweet, the sour smell and the fragrant; the small white violets under the spring hedge, and the snow-white droppings of small birds on the hedge-leaves, were both dear to him. Still more he loved the traditions of the earth you were treading together; the past of the ancient earth of Kent and Wiltshire, or of his native Wales, which he loved better still. Best of all he loved the poets who made their poetry out of these things. On them he threw a light; he threw none on himself, until he also began to make poetry out of what he loved, two years before he died.

Simone de Beauvoir, *The Prime of Life*, trans. Peter Green (1960)

On both sides of the road leading from the station there were restaurants with tables out on the sidewalk, sheltered by high glass screens. I spotted a card in a window which read 'Room to Let'. It was not the kind of room that I particularly liked – it had a vast bed, and chairs, and a wardrobe – but I thought the big table would be useful for working on, and the landlady proposed reasonable *pension* terms. I went back for my case, and left it in the Restaurant de l'Amirauté. Two hours later I had called on the headmistress of my *lycée* and arranged my hours of work. Though I did not know Marseille, I already lived there. Now I set out to explore the town.

I fell in love with it at first sight. I clambered over every rock and ferreted through every back street; I breathed in the smell of tar and dead sea urchins down at the Old Port, mingled with the crowds along the Canebière, and I sat down in tree-lined avenues and public gardens and peaceful little squares where the peculiarly provincial smell of dead leaves eclipsed the sea wind's tang. I loved the clattering trams, with their grapelike clusters of passengers hanging on outside, and names like La Madrague or Mazargue or Les Chartreux or Le Roucas Blanc stuck up in front. On Thursday morning

I rode to Cassis on one of the Mattéi buses: the terminus was quite close to where I lived. I trudged on foot along copper-coloured cliffs all the way from Cassis to La Ciotat, and was so elated by the experience that when I caught the little green bus back that evening all I wanted to do was start off on the same trip again. The passion which caught hold of me then has persisted for over twenty years, and age alone has extinguished it: during those first twelve months it preserved me from boredom, regret, and several sorts of depression, transforming my exile into a holiday.

There was nothing new or surprising about this. The countryside round Marseille was at once wild and easy of access, and held promise of glinting secrets for even the least energetic walker. Such excursions formed the local inhabitants' favourite pastime. The experts joined hiking clubs, and published a regular bulletin with details of various ingenious itineraries. They also carefully maintained the brightly coloured directional arrows that blazed the trail for them along their regular walks. A large number of my colleagues went off together on Sundays to climb the Marseilleveyre massif or the peaks of Sainte-Baume. I was exceptional in that I never attached myself to a group, and managed to turn a pastime into a most exacting duty. Between 2 October and 14 July I never once found myself wondering how to spend my Thursdays and Sundays. I made it a rule to be out of the house by dawn, winter and summer alike, and never to return before nightfall. I didn't bother with all the preliminaries, and never obtained the semi-official rig of rucksack, studded shoes, rough skirt, and wind-cheater. I would slip on an old dress and a pair of espadrilles, and take a few bananas and buns with me in a basket. Sometimes my friends would pass me in the hills, smiling disdainfully. On the other hand, with the aid of the *Bulletin*, the *Guide Bleu*, and a Michelin map, I used to work out my routes to the last detail. At first I limited myself to some five or six hours' walking; then I chose routes that would take nine to ten hours; in time I was doing over twenty-five miles in a day. I worked my way systematically through the entire area: I climbed every peak – Gardaban, Mont Aurélien, Mont Sainte-Victoire, and the Pilon du Roi – and clambered down every gully; I explored every valley, gorge, and defile. On I went, among those white and blinding stones, where there was no hint of path, watching out for the arrows – blue, green, red, or yellow – which led me on I knew not whither. Sometimes I lost track of them and had to hunt round in a circle, thrusting through sharp-scented bushes, scratching myself on various plants which were still new to me: resinaceous rock-roses, juniper, ilex, yellow and white asphodel. I followed all the coastguards' tracks, too; here, at the base of the cliffs, along this racked and indented coast line, the Mediterranean lacked that sweetly languorous calm which so often sickened me when I encountered it elsewhere. In morning splendour it surged fiercely against the headlands, dazzling white, and I felt that if I plunged my hand in I would have my fingers chopped off. It was splendid, too, to watch from the clifftops while with deceptive ease and sheer solid inorganic power it smashed over the breakwaters protecting the olive trees. There came a day in spring, on the Valensole plateau, when I found almond trees in blossom for the first time. I walked along red-and-ochre lanes in the flat country near Aix-en-Provence, and recognized many of Cézanne's canvases. I visited towns large and small, villages, abbeys, and châteaux. As in Spain, my curiosity gave me no respite. I looked for a revelation from each successive hilltop or valley, and always the beauty of the landscape surpassed both my memories and my expectations. With tenacious perseverance I rediscovered my mission to rescue things from oblivion. Alone I walked the mists that hung over the summit of Sainte-Victoire, and strode along the ridge of the Pilon du Roi, bracing myself against a violent wind which sent my beret spinning down into the valley below. Alone again, I got lost in a mountain ravine on the Lubéron range. Such moments, with all their warmth, tenderness, and fury, belong to me and no one else. How I loved to walk through the town while it was still dark, half asleep, and see the dawn come up behind some unknown village! I would take a midday nap with the scent of broom and pine all around me; I would clamber up the flanks of hills and go plodding across open uplands, and things foreseen and unforeseeable would befall me on my way. I never lost the pleasure of finding a dot or some lines upon a map, or three lines entered in my *Guide*, transformed into stones, trees, sky, and water.

Every time I revisit Provence I can see why I love it so much; but these reasons do not adequately explain the mad enthusiasm I felt then – an enthusiasm which I can gauge, with a certain degree of amazement, from one particular memory. Towards the end of November my sister arrived in Marseille, and I initiated her into these new pleasures of mine just as I had done with my childhood games. We saw the Roquefavour aqueduct under a bright midday sun, and ploughed through the snow round Toulon in espadrilles. My sister was unused to such activities; she suffered from agonizing blisters, yet she never complained, and managed to keep up with me. One Thursday – it was midday, and we had just reached Sainte-Baume – she developed a temperature. I told her to lie down in the hospice, have some hot toddy, and wait for the Marseille bus, which was due a few hours later. Then I finished my trek alone. That evening she took to her bed with flu, and I felt a faint twinge of remorse. Today I can scarcely imagine how I could have brought myself to leave her shivering in that gloomy refectory as I did. Generally, it is true, I showed consideration for other people, and I was very fond of my sister. Sartre often used to tell me that I was a schizophrenic, that instead of adapting my schemes to reality I pursued them in the teeth of circumstances, regarding hard facts as something merely peripheral. On Sainte-Baume, in fact, I was prepared to deny my sister's existence rather than deviate from my prepared programme: she had always fallen in so loyally with all my schemes that I refused to envisage the possibility of her disrupting them on this occasion. What Sartre called schizophrenia seemed to me an extreme and aberrant form of my particular brand of optimism. I refused, as I had done when I was twenty, to admit that life contained any wills apart from my own.

The will power that manifested itself in these fanatical walking trips of mine was something very deep-rooted. Long ago in Limousin, as I walked those deep, rutted lanes, I had promised myself that one day I would traverse France, perhaps even the whole world, so thoroughly that I left not one field or thicket unvisited. I did not really believe this; and similarly in Spain, when I claimed that I would see *everything*, I interpreted this word in a decidedly liberal sense. But here, in the limited terrain to which my job and my limited resources restricted me, the claim seemed at least a possible one. I wanted to explore Provence more fully and in a more civilized fashion than any female hiker in herringbone tweed. I had never practised any sport, and therefore took all the more pleasure in driving my body to the very limit of its endurance, by the most ingenious possible methods. To save my energy on the highway I would thumb lifts from cars or trucks; when I was clambering over rocks in the mountains, or sliding down screes, I would work out short cuts, so that each expedition was a work of art in itself. I promised myself to cherish the proud memory of such exploits forever, and in the actual moment of accomplishment I would congratulate myself on my own achievements. The pride which they stirred in me meant that I was forced to repeat them: how could I let myself fall from this high standard? If I had given up even one trip through indifference or to satisfy a mere whim, if I had once asked myself what the point of it all was, I would have destroyed the whole carefully contrived edifice that elevated my pleasures to the level of sacred obligations.

Nan Shepherd, *The Living Mountain* (1977)

At first, mad to recover the tang of height, I made always for the summits, and would not take time to explore the recesses. But late one September I went on Braeriach with a man who knew the hill better than I did then, and he took me aside into Coire an Lochain. One could not have asked a fitter day for the first vision of this rare loch. The equinoctial storms had been severe; snow, that hardly ever fails to powder the plateau about the third week of September, had fallen close and thick, but now the storms had passed, the air was keen and buoyant, with a brilliancy as of ice, the waters of the loch were frost-cold to the fingers. And how still, how incredibly withdrawn and tranquil. Climb as often as you will, Loch Coire an Lochain remains incredible. It cannot be seen until one stands almost on its lip, but only height hides it. Unlike Avon and Etchachan, it is not shut into the mountain but lies on an outer flank, its hollow ranged daily by all the eyes that look at the Caingorms from the Spey. Yet, without knowing, one would not guess its presence and certainly not its size. Two cataracts, the one that feeds it, falling from the brim of the plateau over rock, and the one that drains it, show as white threads on the mountain. Having scrambled up the bed of the latter (not, as I knew later, the simple way, but my companion was a rabid naturalist who had business with every leaf, stalk and root in the rocky bed), one expects to be near the corrie, but no, it is still a long way off. And on one toils, into the hill. Black scatter of rock, pieces large as a house, pieces edged like a grater. A tough bit of going. And there at last is the loch, held tight back against the precipice. Yet as I turned, that September day, and looked back through the clean air, I could see straight out to ranges of distant hills. And that astonished me. To be so open and yet so secret! Its anonymity – Loch of the Corrie of the Loch, that is all – seems to guard this surprising secrecy. Other lochs, Avon, Morlich and the rest, have their distinctive names. One expects of them an idiosyncrasy. But Loch of the Corrie of the Loch, what could there be? A tarn like any other. And then to find this distillation of loveliness!

I put my fingers in the water and found it cold. I listened to the waterfall until I no longer heard it. I let my eyes travel from shore to shore very slowly and was amazed at the width of the water. How could I have foreseen so large a loch, 3,000-odd feet up, slipped away into this corrie which was only one of three upon one face of a mountain that was itself only a broken bit of the plateau? And a second time I let my eyes travel over the surface, slowly, from shore to shore, beginning at my feet and ending against the precipice. There is no way like that for savouring the extent of a water surface.

This changing of focus in the eye, moving the eye itself when looking at things that do not move, deepens one's sense of outer reality. Then static things may be caught in the very act of becoming. By so simple a matter, too, as altering the position of one's head, a different kind of world may be made to appear. Lay the head down, or better still, face away from what you look at, and bend with straddled legs till you see your world upside down. How new it has become! From the close-by sprigs of heather to the most distant fold of the land, each detail stands erect in its own validity. In no other way have I seen of my own unaided sight that the earth is round. As I watch, it arches its back, and each layer of landscape bristles – though *bristles* is a word of too much commotion for it. Details are no longer part of a grouping in a picture of which I am the focal point, the focal point is everywhere. Nothing has reference to me, the looker. This is how the earth must see itself.

Jenny Nimmo, *The Snow Spider* (1986)

They finished the dishes in silence. Then, with the wind and his ancestors filling his thoughts, Gwyn rushed upstairs and opened the drawer. But he did not remove the seaweed. The first thing he noticed was the brooch, lying on top of the scarf. He could not remember having replaced it that way. Surely the scarf was the last thing he had returned to the drawer?

The sunlight, slanting through his narrow window, fell directly on to the brooch and the contorted shapes slowly assumed the form of a star, then a snowflake, next a group of petals changed into a creature with glittering eyes before becoming a twisted piece of metal again. Something or somebody wanted him to use the brooch!

Gwyn picked it up and thrust it into his pocket. Grabbing his anorak from a chair he rushed downstairs and out of the back door. He heard a voice, as he raced across the yard, calling him to a chore. 'But the wind was too loud, wasn't it?' he shouted joyfully to the sky. 'I never heard nothing!'

He banged the yard gate to emphasise his words and began to run through the field; after a hundred yards the land began to rise; he kept to the sheeptrack for a while, then climbed a wall and jumped down into another field, this one steep and bare. He was among the sheep now, scattering them as he bounded over mounds and boulders. Stopping at the next wall, he took a deep breath. The mountain had begun in earnest. Now it had to be walking or climbing, running was impossible.

A sense of urgency gripped him; an overwhelming feeling that today, perhaps within that very hour, something momentous would occur.

He stumbled on, now upon a sheeptrack, now heaving himself over boulders. He had climbed the mountain often, sometimes with Alun, sometimes alone, but the first time had been with Bethan, one summer long ago. It had seemed an impossible task then, when he was not five years old, but she had willed him to the top, comforting and cajoling him with her gentle voice. 'It's so beautiful when you get there, Gwyn. You can see the whole world, well the whole of Wales anyway, and the sea, and clouds below you. You won't fall, I won't let you!' She had been wearing the yellow scarf that day. Gwyn remembered how it had streamed out across his head, like a banner, when they reached the top.

It was not a high mountain, nor a dangerous one, some might even call it a hill. It was wide and grassy, a series of gentle slopes that rose, one after another, pattered with drystone walls and windblown bushes. The plateau at the top was a lonely place, however. From here only the empty fields and surrounding mountains could be seen and, far out to the west, the distant grey line of the sea. Gwyn took shelter beside the tallest rock, for the wind sweeping across the plateau threatened to roll him back whence he had come.

He must surely have found the place to offer his brooch. 'Give it to the wind,' Nain had said. Bracing himself against the rock, Gwyn extended his up-turned hand into the wind and uncurled his fingers.

The brooch was snatched away so fast that he never saw what became of it. He withdrew his hand and waited for the wind to answer, not knowing what the answer would be, but wanting it to bring him something that would change the way things were, to fill the emptiness in the house below.

But the wind did not reply. It howled about Gwyn's head and tore at his clothes, then slowly it died away taking, somewhere within its swirling streams and currents, the precious brooch, and leaving nothing in return.

Then, from the west, came a silver-white cloud of snow, obscuring within minutes the sea, the surrounding mountains and the fields below. And, as the snow began to encircle and embrace him, Gwyn found himself chanting, 'Math, Lord of Gwynedd, Gwydion and Gilfaethwy!' This he repeated, over and over again, not knowing whether he was calling to the living or the dead. And all the while, huge snowflakes drifted silently about him, melting as they touched him, so that he did not turn into the snowman that he might otherwise have become.

Gwyn stood motionless for what seemed like hours, enveloped in a soft, serene whiteness, waiting for an answer. Yet, had Nain promised him an answer? In the stillness he thought he heard a sound, very high and light, like icicles on glass.

His legs began to ache, his face grew numb with cold and, when night clouds darkened the sky, he began his descent, resentful and forlorn.

The lower slopes of the mountain were still green, the snow had not touched them and it was difficult for Gwyn to believe he had been standing deep in snow only minutes earlier. Only from the last field could the summit be seen, but by the time Gwyn reached the field the mountain was obscured by mist, and he could not tell if snow still lay above.

It was dark when he got home. Before opening the back door he stamped his boots. His absence from the farm all day would not be appreciated, he realized, and he did not wish to aggravate the situation with muddy boots. He raised his hand to brush his shoulders free of the dust he usually managed to collect, and his fingers encountered something icy cold.

Believing it to be a snowflake or even an icicle, Gwyn plucked it off his shoulder and moved closer to the kitchen window to examine what he had found. His mother had not yet drawn the curtains and light streamed into the yard.

It was a snowflake; the most beautiful he had ever seen, for it was magnified into an exquisite and intricate pattern: a star glistening like crystal in the soft light. And then the most extraordinary thing happened. The star began to move and Gwyn stared amazed as it gradually assumed the shape of a tiny silver spider. Had the wind heard him after all? Was he a magician then?

Alexandra Stewart, *Daughters of the Glen* (1986)

All his life my father seemed to preserve the doting eye that poets share with little children. I don't believe he was ever bored in his own countryside from the early days as a herd boy. There was always something to watch, some association to remember, changes in light and sound and fragments of poetry and local lore to think about. A well-stored mind is its own good company and long hours spent walking were not time wasted as they could be to mechanised armies nowadays who can't enjoy what they are passing because they've timed themselves to be somewhere else as soon as possible.

From Woodend to Tulchan is a marvellous walk – all the better then when the roads were smooth and white and soft as velvet to bare feet in the cart tracks, free of the noise of engines on the ground or in the air, and no smells of petroleum or rubber to get up your nose. I like to think of my father setting out on a bright morning in the late spring, a long lifetime ago – the dew still on the grass, for he was an early riser.

He would start walking down the road into the morning sun, with the woods of Creag Mhor on the left and the big field of his own croft on the right, above the river, past the Iron Well and the widening of the road where Queen Victoria's carriage turned on a jaunt from Taymouth Castle in 1842 and then by the winding road carved out of the sheer sides of the Pass of Glenlyon, with the mortared walls above a drop of a couple of hundred feet that generations of reckless children have walked along. The road follows the river on a sharp turn to the right when it comes into the Dale of Fortingall and then bears left, while father would take the footpath beside the river, broad, shallow and sauntering over gravel beaches after its foaming hurry through the rocks of the pass. Across the water the steadings of Culdaremore farm catch the morning sun; in the other direction lie the thatch roofs of Fortingall village, the parkland round Glenlyon House and the broad meadows by the river where everyone always believed there had once been a Roman camp, and some folk also believe that Pontius Pilate was born.

After a few hundred yards, he would cross the Lyon Bridge, and walk south by the little saddle between the foothills of the Lawers ridge and Drummond Hill to Fearnan, while the Lyon made another sharp turn to the left for a five-mile amble round the other side of Drummond Hill to join the Tay in the strath beyond Keltneyburn. On the Fearnan road he would enjoy again the first of many fine views of Loch Tay as he rounded the shoulder of the hill – a broad expanse of water among the woods and hills, curving out of sight to the west, and with a steamer – maybe two steamers – on it, for the loch itself was a busy waterway in those days. On foot or horse-drawn to Fearnan, by steamer to Killin and then by train to Glasgow was our most familiar journey south. The steamer service finally ended during the Second World War, and for years there was little more than a few rowing boats on the loch, although now there is a marina at Kenmore and a lot of other boating.

From Fearnan to Kenmore is a three-mile walk between woods of Drummond Hill and the loch shore, by a road that is now fast and frequented. Eighty years ago there were more people about the place, most of them hard-working as they had to be, but fast road traffic was still in the future. In the spring there was a chorus of bird song all the way to the bridge where the river Tay flowed out of the loch past the model village put up at Kenmore by the Campbells of Breadalbane at the height of their wealth beside one of the great gates to their mansion of Taymouth Castle.

Beyond Kenmore the walker takes the hill road to the south, a steep climb with hairpin bends past the old cottage at Tombuie towards Glen Quaich and Loch Freuchie. The parting view of Loch Tay is splendid again, and about four miles up on the moor, there is a 2,000 ft. peak from which you can see the entire Lawers ridge and nort-eastward to Schiehallion and the lower ridge that runs up to the north of Strathtay to Pitlochry. Away to the west is the steep peak of Ben More. It was still possible then to quote the old *Punch* rhyme:

From Kenmore to Ben More the land is all
    the Marquis's.

For years now, of course, the huge estates of the Marquises of Breadalbane have been no more than a memory.

A little further on the walker gets a first glimpse of Loch Freuchie, particularly dear to my father because of its connection with the legend of Fraoch which won him his Mod gold medal before I was born. He was also familiar with the mass emigration that had emptied the little glen a couple of generations before, when almost everyone left in one group for Canada. Here the old drove road drops steeply – 600 feet in less than a mile; with a tarred surface for some years now, it is still too much for some cars.

Another five miles or so, past the south shore of the little loch, and the walker turns south towards Wade's road about a mile from Amulree – 'Ford of Maelrubha', the seventh-century missionary whose name is found in place names from Perthshire to Sutherland. His name means 'the red monk', and it is sometimes difficult to know whether a place is named for him or for Mary.

Maelrubha gave his name to Loch Maree in the far north-west and set up a famous sanctuary for fugitives at Applecross, the Ross-shire parish that I came to know so well during the Second World War.

Away to the west the walker sees the big, rounded hills that reach over 3,000 feet in Ben Chonzie and to the east Strathbraan runs between the moors to Dunkeld. Another three or four miles to the south and we reach Newton Bridge where the road makes a ninety degree turn to the left and follows the River Almond through the Sma' Glen; there the river meanders along the floor of the deep valley with the precipitous sides that it has cut through the southern rim of the Highlands. Although it is barely two miles long, the Sma' Glen must have been a fierce-looking entrance to the Caledonians' stronghold in the old days, when there was a fort on Dun Mor and the valley floor was thick with trees and scrub.

The Romans had a lookout station at Fendoch, at the southern entrance to the Sma' Glen. Perhaps they ventured no farther north. In spite of the tradition that there was a Roman camp at Fortingall, no excavation has turned up any Roman remains there.

In the Sma' Glen also is Clach Ossian, a stone marking some association with the great bard – it would be a bold one who would claim to know where he was born or buried among all the places claiming a connection.

For a man like my father, this walk would be alive with the lore and legend of nearly two thousand years, and the activity all about him of his own time, which was much more populous than now, and fifty years before had been more populous still. If you retrace that walk today, you will find ruins that were new buildings when Alastair Stewart passed that way to collect the white cow.

Muriel Gray, *The First Fifty: Munro-Bagging Without a Beard* (1991)

You remember your first mountain in much the same way you remember having your first sexual experience except that walking doesn't make as much mess and you don't cry for a week if Ben Nevis forgets to phone the next morning.

But, like losing your virginity, it's hard to recreate that nascent flavour of exhilaration when you realize that by determination, corporeal suffering that involves wheezing until your lungs feel like a laboratory beagle's, you've done something you didn't believe physically possible. Unfortunately, unlike losing your virginity, Munro-bagging stays just as sore every time you do it.

To the sofa-bound layperson it may just be a wind-blown cairn, grey and dismal except for its decorative orange peel, but to you it's nirvana. It remains constantly awe-inspiring that your feet, and a flask of tomato soup, can take you to the remotest and most primevally beautiful parts of our country, from where those who sit in aluminium chairs a foot from an open hatchback listening to Gary Davis's *Bit In the Middle* are excluded by their sedentary nature. It's a sensation that once felt has to be repeated for the rest of your life, or until the end of Gary Davis's *Bit In the Middle*, whichever comes first.

Ben Arthur, or The Cobbler, was my first. Not a Munro, but 15 years ago, at the tender age of 16 when I should have been in Sauchiehall Street choosing stripey socks, I could be forgiven for never having heard of Sir Hugh or his damned tables. Never mind Munros – had I known how hard The Cobbler was to be I would have stayed home and watched a black-and-white movie on telly with my mum. To this day I am the kind of hill-walker who starts the day with a face like a football with slits cut in it for eyes. The early start so essential to claiming that peak has never become easier. But to impress the man I loved at the time, I emerged from his friend's beat-up Mini at the car park opposite Arrochar thinking, 'I am not going to lose this very handsome boyfriend who wants to do this instead of going to Kelvingrove Art Gallery for a look at the Rembrandt and a snog. I will die as soon as we start to walk.'

'He's bound to leave me to rot,' I surmised, 'and get off with that tart from the textiles department at Glasgow School of Art that seemed to fancy him. I'll bet she goes hill-walking,' I thought as I caught sight of my figure in a donkey jacket and waterproof trousers in the car's wing mirror. Mind you, with thighs like a Tyrannosaurus Rex I suppose the brazen hussy would have been well suited to the hills, and I bet even her hair would mat like felt under a balaclava for eight hours.

So I admit it was sex that drove me on that winter's day, through rain at first, turning to sleet as we passed the tree line and into wet driving snow as we neared the top.

Winter hill-climbing has tortures all of its own. Never go first in thick snow unless you have legs that are six feet long and thighs of iron. Breaking the path is murder. For some reason I imagined this was my task, kicking pathetic little holes up the gradient with all the effectiveness of a toddler having a tantrum in a supermarket.

In those days of misplaced student feminism I was terrified of being seen as a feeble girlie. God knows why. These days I'd sing *On the Good Ship Lollipop* and speak like Bonnie Langford if I could get one of the lazy bastards with beards to carry my rucksack. Unfortunately, 20th-century men are shrewd, reserving their manly acts of chivalry only for those who resemble Brooke Shields. Since my hair does indeed mat like felt under a balaclava, I usually end up carrying their rucksacks.

But, way back then, I genuinely believed that physical weakness was a sign of inferiority, and so I would struggle away, silently hyperventilating to keep up with those men who weighed 13 stone next to my eight stone, and whose legs were so big they could get to the top in three strides.

Wrestling with the thought 'I want to go back' is fundamental to hill-walking, and of course all the bearded experts with accents like Sussex vicars will advise you that you must always know when to turn back. If you are 16 and trying to get your boyfriend to think you're great, the answer is that you may only turn back when all the other members of the party before you have lost two or more of their limbs and decide it's time to call it a day.

I imagined it with horror.

'I see you've lost a leg there, Ian.'

'Aye, Alec, but it's OK. It's only knocked the schedule out by ten minutes. We'll be at the top in an hour. How's that grievous spinal injury you've just incurred?'

'No problem, Ian. I'll just crawl up to this coll with my one good arm and take a bearing. Is that Ladhar Bheinn over there or are the severe facial lacerations I have been unlucky enough to receive clouding my vision? Any Lucozade left?'

This too has changed in my maturity. Now I make sure we travel in my car. There is no greater incentive for calling the shots than cheerily telling the chaps who want to continue up a mountain in a force-ten gale and blizzard that they may make their own way back from Torridon to Glasgow.

However, I digress. Struggling up The Cobbler as I was on that day, I was not only wrestling with the thought 'I want to go back', I had started to form the thought 'Perhaps I'll die'. The worst aspect of this thought at 16 is that Mountain Rescue may remove your balaclava before you've got to a hair brush. 'Nasty,' the mountain leader would say. 'Hair matted like felt.'

But no-one had explained the pain barrier to me at that age. It is the most astonishing feeling, that only someone as chronically unfit as I am can experience, to come through the painful fog into the bright sunlight of new energy. The medical explanation is to do with metabolism and stamina. My explanation is that I remembered there were to be pork pies soon. The arrival at the top of that small hill meant everything to me. Not only lunch and a chance to sit down on a rock, but the fact that in spite of my grossly sedentary nature, I was actually there on the snowy summit with the boys.

What could have been more thrilling and rewarding than to have conquered pain, exhaustion and the humiliation of looking like a navigational engineer, to stand on this beautiful, silent top drinking in the view across Loch Long to Ben Lomond? I was elated, and have continued to be every time I haul myself to the summit of anything higher than the top deck of a bus.

It seems ludicrous now that I found such a short walk so arduous. But it's important to realize that most teenage girls take exercise only when dancing round their handbags at discos looking for men over six foot. Stamina is often psychological and if you wander the Munros in all seasons, you'll find yourself calling on it in a bewildering variety of situations.

I'm grateful that it was a boyfriend who gave me that first taste of the hills, and not my parents. I often come across small family units wandering through the heather, a tweedy university lecturer of a father setting the pace, followed at a respectful distance by a bespectacled, lank-haired mother wearing an acrylic hat and towing two sulky miserable children. Judging by their disgruntled demeanour, these poor mites will doubtless stop walking the hills the moment they grow their first pubic hair, and I grieve for all the pleasure they will miss as adults if they put the hills aside as one would childhood caravan holidays in Girvan. Only take your children up mountains if they beg and scream to go. A pleasure you discover for yourself is worth far more than one you were expected to enjoy by your elders. And how can you enjoy a cold pint in the bar afterwards if you're only seven and a half?

Apart from anything else, hill-walking is not quite as wholesome as your bearded, Fair Isle tank-top brigade would have us believe, so exposing your children to some of the tartan-shirted bears one finds relieving themselves behind cairns is perhaps to be avoided.

So The Cobbler got me going and I haven't stopped since.

Kathleen Jamie, 'At Point of Ness', from *The Queen of Sheba* (1994)

The golf course shifts
uneasily beside the track
where streetlight melts
to a soft frontier with winter dark.
I cross, then, helpless as a ship,
must let night load me, before
moving on between half-sensed
dry-stane walls; day-birds tucked in some nook.

Tonight, the darkness roars.
Even the fishermen's
Nissen hut seems to breathe
beside its spawn of creels,
a dreadful beaching. I walk on,
toward the shore, where night's
split open, the entire
archipelago set as sink-weight
to the sky. A wind's

caught me now; breath frosts,
and I count, to calm me, the Sound's

lighthouses as they shine and fade
across the surge. Graemsay
beams a long systolic five
to one of dark; Hoy a distant
two: two; scattered buoys
blink where skerries drown, then cut
to sea and stars, then
bloom again, weird lilies
wilt and bloom, till
heart-scared, I have it
understood:

   never   *ever*
harm – this,

     you never could

and run – that constant roar,
the track's black vein; toward salt
lit windows, my own door . . .

      Sunshine
gleams the dry-stane dykes'
lovely melanoma of lichen. A wren
flicks on a weathered post
like a dud lighter, by the track
that splits the golf course
from the town's edge to the shore,
where I walk this afternoon
for a breath of air.

Alice Oswald, 'Another Westminster Bridge', from *Woods, etc.* (2005)

go and glimpse the lovely inattentive water
discarding the gaze of many a bored street walker

where the weather trespasses into strip-lit offices
through tiny windows into tiny thoughts
    and authorities

and the soft beseeching tapping of typewriters

take hold of a breath-width instant, stare
at water which is already elsewhere
in a scrapwork of flashes and glittery flutters
and regular waves of apparently motionless motion

under the teetering structures of administration

where a million shut-away eyes glance once
restlessly at the river's ruts and glints

count five, then wander swiftly
away over the stone wing-bone of the city

Gwyneth Lewis, 'Imaginary Walks in Istanbul', from *Sparrow Tree* (2011)

I

It's time I make my daily promenade
to nowhere special – round the footstool
and parlour. Just as Søren Kierkegaard

and father took imaginary strolls
inside looking out, not needing travel.
I apologise now to Istanbul –

never been there – but I find myself full
of mosques and ferries, crosses and crusades,
a journey that's purely fictional.

I've drunk cool sherbert and lemonade
in Bosphorus villas: quarters of mind.
Untaken photographs will never fade

because they're unreal. I want a dervish,
Neck broken, to spin like a radar dish.

2

Let's start with omphalos, the empire's O
In Hagia Sofia, a porphyry
Belly-button that was Justinian's throne.

(Ignore Anonymous of Banduri
On the marble columns, he's full of shit.)
Upstairs, Christ holds a digital TV

Like legal tablets. Notice that he squints,
One eye on me, one on eternity
And he won't stop looking, so that I split

Apart like an atom. From out the frieze
Birds fly, wings bladed, the doorways' veils
Are torn to shreds by the slasher breeze,

A cathedral apocalypse: vermeil
And glass chandeliers explode to shrapnel.

3

The hidden contents of the ottoman.
We could slide down its armrest, and we did,
Often, its dark brown Victorian oilskin

Was slippery enough – I'd bump my head
Each time. In other moods, I'd count and thumb
The rosary of upholstery studs

Along the edge. By now you know that I'm
A counter, and I do admire a square
With something in it. My buttocks would numb

If I read on it – no give in horsehair
So thin. But the syllables from the east
Intrigued me. I loved this backless chair,

A hard place, not designed for rest.
My whole life's secreted inside this chest.

4

The Great Ones left evidence everywhere:
Not far from the Halberdiers-with-Tresses
You'll find a casket containing the hair

Of the Prophet Muhammed. May you gaze
On his tooth, his footprint, admire the hem
Of the Holy Mantle. The guidebook says

That the delightful Circumcision Room
Is not to be missed – go back if it's full.
Check out the Saucepan of Ibrahim.

What's 'like the apple but not the apple?'
A pear? Ram's testicles. Look how the crease
Between sweetbreads is perfect, the pouches full

Of goodness. Each night leaves a cicatrice
On my face. By day, it heals without trace.

5

A language in which the point of the i
Is optional must be admired. I rate
Such subtlety – the disposed-of housefly,

The cauterised mole. I hallucinate
ts without crosses (not the same as l).
You can count me out of the caliphate

That's coming. Not because I'm infidel
But my fid is other and my style
Non-fanatic. My headquarters are smell,

Rotting melon. Goat shit's a spiritual
Discipline if your dogma's maggots,
From whose prophetic writhings one might tell

Who goes to hell, who doesn't. High carrots
And lilies ooze tea. I believe those dots.

6

Last turn's to the Church of Constantine Lips,
which had seven apses and three narthex,
most unusual. Like the brain's lop-

sided map of the body: monstrous sex,
slight neck, a set of negligible limbs,
spatula fingertips – the practical codex

of how life feels. In the park by Taksim
Square: 'Madame, I am not a cannibal,
I merely wish to sell you a kilim

from my native province.' And, like a fool,
I let him. There are no silent letters
in Turkish, and he was so affable . . .

My tours, you'll note, have contained no errors
But getting lost is what guidebooks are for.

Cheryl Strayed, *Wild: A Journey from Lost to Found* (2012)

I slept finally that night in the woods somewhere outside the Whitehorse Campground. And when I did, I dreamed of snow. Not the snow in which my brother and I had killed Lady, but the snow I'd just passed through up in the mountains, the memory of it more frightening than the experience of it had been. All night long, I dreamed of the things that could have happened but didn't. Skidding and sliding down a treacherous slope and off the side of a cliff or crashing into rocks below. Walking and never coming to that road, but wandering lost and starving instead.

I studied my guidebook as I ate my breakfast the next morning. If I walked up to the PCT as planned, I'd be walking into more snow. The idea of that spooked me, and as I gazed at my map I saw that I didn't have to do it. I could walk back to the Whitehorse Campground and west farther still to Bucks Lake. From there I could follow a jeep road that wended its way north, ascending to the PCT at a place called Three Lakes. The alternate route was about the same distance as the PCT, approximately fifteen miles, but it was at a low enough elevation that it had a chance of being snow-free. I packed up my camp, walked back down the trail I'd come on the night before, and strode defiantly through the Whitehorse Campground.

All morning, as I walked west to Bucks Lake, then north and west again along its shore before coming to the rugged jeep road that would take me back up to the PCT, I thought of the resupply box that waited for me in Belden Town. Not so much the box, but the twenty-dollar bill that would be inside. And not so much the twenty-dollar bill, but the food and beverages I could buy with it. I spent hours in a half-ecstatic, half-tortured reverie, fantasizing about cake and cheeseburgers, chocolate and bananas, apples and mixed-green salads, and, more than anything, about Snapple lemonade. This did not make sense. I'd had only a few Snapple lemonades in my pre-PCT life and liked them well enough, but they hadn't stood out in any particular way. It had not been *my drink*. But now it haunted me. Pink or yellow, it didn't matter. Not a day passed that I didn't imagine in vivid detail what it would be like to hold one in my hand and bring it to my mouth. Some days I forbade myself to think about it, lest I go entirely insane.

I could see that the road to Three Lakes had only recently become free of snow. Great gashes had split open in places across it and streams of melting snow flowed in wide gaping gullies along its sides. I followed it up beneath a dense canopy of trees without seeing anyone. Midafternoon, I felt a familiar tug inside me. I was getting my period, I realized. My first on the trail. I'd almost forgotten it could come. The new way I'd been aware of my body since beginning my hike had blunted the old ways. No longer was I concerned about the delicate intricacies of whether I felt infinitesimally fatter or thinner than I had the day before. There was no such thing as a bad hair day. The smallest inner reverberations were obliterated by the frank pain I always felt in the form of my aching feet or the muscles of my shoulders and upper back that knotted and burned so hard and hot that I had to pause several times an hour to do a series of moves that would offer a moment of relief. I took off my pack, dug through my first aid kit, and found the jagged hunk of natural sponge I'd put in a small ziplock bag before my trip began. I'd used it only a few times experimentally before I took it on the PCT. Back in Minneapolis, the sponge had seemed like a sensible way to deal with my period given my circumstances on the trail, but now that I held it, I was less than sure. I attempted to wash my hands with water from my bottle, dousing the sponge as I did so, and then squeezed it out, pulled down my shorts, squatted on the road, and pushed the sponge into my vagina as far as I could, wedging it against my cervix.

Linda Cracknell, *Doubling Back: Ten Paths Trodden in Memory* (2014)

Those first days in September when I set out from Perthshire were the year's summer. Squadrons of dragonflies hummed around my head, scabious and meadowsweet brushed my bare calves, and the air was still, sweetened with birdsong. My familiar places close to home sprang up – bright cold pools I sometimes swim in, birch tunnels I cycle through, local ways up Carn Gorm or Ben Lawers. When I break a cycle ride or an autumn walk at the Post Office at Bridge of Balgie, delicate cups are delivered upon flowered saucers and filled and refilled with tea.

This start in a familiar landscape joined up my day walks, gave me the pleasure of naming places, but also noticing the shifts in colour, and the slow changes in the bulky shape of Ben Lawers as I skirted its sides. It was strange but lovely that for the first two nights I was near enough home to stay with local friends.

After three golden days in Glen Lyon, the wind rose, cloud lowered and I had my first night camping, with the river rumbling past my tent just downstream from Pubil dam. I walked the first half of that day with friends Sue and Iain who met me at the dam. We walked west past Loch Lyon, dammed up and bleak without trees, untouched by tarmac, and leading up into a confluence of high glens. The turrets of the fortress that arcs northeast from Beinn Dorain in the south to Beinn a Creachain, had walled me out of the 'beyond' by this route until now. Then the others had to turn back and we said our goodbyes.

The slight rise of Glen Meran took me northwards, hair dampening as I climbed into mist, feet following where the deer had trodden paths. The weight of my rucksack gnawed an ache deep into my hip joints. In the late afternoon, Glen Meran spilt me onto Rannoch Moor. My eyes sought features on the blank bog: pylons stalking along the Fort William railway line; an occasional Scots Pine isolating itself as a dark silhouette, flattened by dull light. I followed a quad bike trail to find the 'creep', a low gap under the embanked railway. My feet were pulled at by gloopy peat bog. In crazed fluorescence, green and red mosses caught at my eye as if displaced from a world of coral reefs. I abandoned the preserve of dry boots and socks. For the first time on the walk I was out of my comfort zone, wet and peat-splattered, travelling very slowly in an unknown land.

Alone, the meshing of rhythm, thought and observation had me inventing songs and rhymes. Lyrics were delivered in my head to the tune of *Walking on the Moon* by The Police.

'I hope your legs don't break
Walking Rannoch Moor.
A boat's what you should take
Walking Rannoch Moor.'

And so on. Another long-distance solo walker I've come across imagined he was a bearer of news between families of cows separated by long distance. When they rushed over to the fence to meet him it was as if he was a mail-ship arriving. He passed on news of Sister Agnes's sore nipples and so on. The mind plays games when left to talk to itself, and for my part I enjoy this slightly off-beat creativity.

I spent that night in a bothy I came across by chance by the Water of Tulla. In the morning, sun blasted the valley into a tumble of white rock and blue river and outlined the beckoning hills of the west. I took everything outside to dry on the grass and stood by my front door. The rattle of the train to Fort William approached, growing into a gallop opposite me, and then steadying on its looping journey north. I imagined how I must look from the train, a wifie outside her cottage, miles from anywhere.

I descended towards Loch Tulla, breathing in heather scent as the hills cleared of cloud ahead of me. I hailed the hooked peak of Stob Ghabhar that I'd climbed on a day of hard snow and sun a couple of winters before. Only half an hour later I reached something else familiar at my left shoulder; a climb with friends up Ben Achaladair about 15 years before. I remembered how in the first few morning miles we had dallied through the Black Wood of Crannach which sits grandly under Beinn a' Creachain. Later, caught out by early snow and the change from British Summer Time, we'd ended up benighted and slithering through wet snow and peat bog, pulled by two dogs on leads towards lights in the valley. Today I looked at the wood from the other side of the river, sunlight highlighting the shelves of Scots Pine foliage.

The line of the walk was taking me out of familiarity and then returning me to it. Crossing thresholds and linking places. I took notice when I read in Thomas A Clark's poem *In Praise of Walking*: 'We can walk between two places and in so doing establish a link between them, bring them into a warmth of contact, like introducing two friends.' I'd come to walk the drovers' route, but perhaps it had partly appealed to me because of this linking of memories.

A heron at the edge of the water caught my eye. Then an electronic bleep stopped me; I had walked back into mobile phone territory. The phone had hung on to a message sent sometime between days two and five, between Glen Lyon and Glen Tulla. It was from my Edinburgh friend Kathy Jarvis who I've walked and climbed many Scottish hills with. She's passionate about the high Andes and runs a trekking business there, but I knew she'd be setting out on a brand new adventure during my time away.

Her message read: 'Lewis Jarvis born ten am today! All well! x'

I whispered a Hurrah for Kathy and for Lewis, mentally threading another bright jewel on my string of journey-beads. This one though seemed misted with a little sadness. The heron mobilised its elbowing wings, took off and soared upstream.

Linda Cracknell, 'Assynt's Rare Animals?' (2015)

In May this year I climbed Quinag for the first time. I had saved its magnificence for such a day; recently raucous south-westerlies had stilled and cloud flurried high above the summits. Threading through its towers and buttresses, gaping clefts and chutes of long, vertical scree, I felt I was touring the walls of an ancient castle. Its giant proportions invited a very different view from each of three peaks. The human footprint was scant on the land I looked down on, save for the sparkle of white cottages clinging to headlands and coasts. The ribbon-road towards Lochinver was forced to twist between archipelagos of lochs and lochans, and solitary hills thrust up at absurd angles in triumphant resistance to the ice age which had scoured away fathoms of sandstone once submerging them.

Assynt, Midsummer 1979. My first visit to Scotland. I came in a minibus of students from Exeter College of Art, staying for a week at a hostel in the village of Elphin. After the green hills and cream-tea-cosiness of Devon, I was shocked by this bare, rock-heaving place that had taken two days to reach and flaunted its indifference to our efforts. I recall an impression of rock and corrugated iron; of tipped up hills and water; of sunburn, rain, wind, white sand beaches and explorations which rarely led to a shop or a tearoom. This, I discovered, was somewhere where I could walk and be seriously alone; where the mountains shoved the past into my present, and the yawn of land between Elphin and the coast seemed to out-wild the entire rugged mass of Dartmoor, my local 'wilderness'. At this charmed time of year so far north, nature never rested, continuing about its gurgling, twittering, groaning business as we wrestled with sleep.

The area thrilled and, in equal measure, unnerved me. Since then I've returned often to Assynt and Coigach to climb, walk and cycle in all seasons. Each time I've been re-prickled by the same awe, but a sense of savagery has been tempered by laying out my own lines of memory cairns: camping spots, blizzard-blinded hills, the various people I've come here with; memories now reawakened as I gaze across it from unforgiving Quinag.

It's impossible not to feel something primal as a walker here; to shrink against space and the pulse of deep geological time. In two visits this year, in May and at Midsummer, I've trodden my superficial way across the palimpsest. It's underpinned by rock formations dating back over 3,000 million years; by finding that Clachtoll has strayed here from the equator; by the knowledge that bear, reindeer, lynx, arctic fox, wolves and even polar bear roamed here if we dream back over 45,000 years prompted by remains found at the Inchnadamph Bone Caves.

Stories of more recent human settlement and exile lie in the topmost layers, remembered by the moss-coated piles of stone on remnant pasture and silenced cattle. The depopulation of the 19th century saw 48 communities in Assynt emptied of their inhabitants according to the Napier Commission, many people departing the country or ending up in coastal townships such as Clachtoll. Pausing there as I walked north towards the coastal broch, I came across a monument to the charismatic Reverend Norman MacLeod who emigrated to Canada in 1817 trailing after him a stream of 'Normanites'. They spent more than 30 years in Canada and then, clocking up a sail of 14,000 miles, he settled with his 800 followers in Waipu, New Zealand in 1853. 'They followed him to the ends of the earth,' the monument recalls.

Since 1979 I've witnessed change here myself, excited this spring by the fluorescent spring flush of regenerating thickets of birch and hazel, by paths in remote areas that are accessible even by wheelchair, and new businesses. The buyout of the 21,000 acre North Assynt Estate by its crofters in 1993 set a precedent and further community buyouts followed, including in 2005 Glencanisp and Dumrunie Estates, and the purchase of Quinag by the John Muir Trust. New patterns in land ownership have led to new priorities: native woodland expansion, upgraded paths, enrichment of people's lives and the local economy. The Coigach-Assynt Living Landscapes initiative is one of the largest landscape restoration projects in Europe, creating amongst other things, a tree nursery at Little Assynt maintaining oak, birch, rowan, hazel, scots pine, holly and wych elm of local provenance for planting.

A cool spring and early summer this year, especially in this top left corner of Scotland, meant everything was happening at once – cuckoos whooped manically; violets, primroses, bluebells, orchids, yellow flags fraternised promiscuously alongside paths; a solitary black throated diver had taken up its liveried residence in Achmelvich Bay . . .

In June I walked here with my old friend Sonia. Cloud sank onto the hills and we took low-level and coastal routes, carving a rough figure of eight across the 1:50,000 Loch Assynt map: Lochinver, Achmelvich, Drumbeg, Loch Assynt (through Glen Leireag under the wrinkled cliff of Quinag's Sail Gorm), Lochinver and its famous pies again, Achiltibuie and finally back to Ullapool via Strathcannaird on the 'postie's path'. I enjoyed a sense of joining up the dots, etching with our feet a connected route (even when this meant walking several miles on the road to Drumbeg into the tidal roar of Germany's Alfa Romeo club!).

For much of our route we were revisiting known paths – the bog-myrtle-scented soars and plummets between Lochinver and Achmelvich; the postie's path whose seriousness had caught us out in peat-splattered darkness at midwinter 20 years before – but the weather always crafted a new character for our old ways. At first we were clammed in by cloud, heads in a helmet of bird chatter. Then the summer solstice offered Aegean clarity as we walked the coast between Achmelvich and Stoer Lighthouse. Each rise over a headland offered a fresh arrangement of rock, white sand, turquoise inlet, until the dramatic sloping beds and sheer gulf of Clachtoll's split rock heralded an ancient boundary underfoot – 3 billion-year old Lewissian gneiss to the east meeting Torridonian sandstone a third its age. On another day, harsh north-easterlies roiled the sea into a black-green cauldron around the beach at Clashnessie and we walked, heads bent, into a whole new season.

Lauren Elkin, *Flâneuse: Women Walk the City in Paris, New York, Tokyo, Venice and London* (2016)

In my ignorance, I think I thought I invented *flânerie*. Coming from suburban America, where people drive from one place to another, walking for no particular reason was a bit of an eccentric thing to do. I could walk for hours in Paris and never 'get' anywhere, looking at the way the city was put together, glimpsing its unofficial history here and there, a bullet in the facade of an *hôtel particulier*, leftover stencilling way up on the side of a building for a flour company or a newspaper that no longer existed (which some inspired graffiti artist had used as an invitation to add his own work) or a row of cobblestones revealed by roadworks, several layers below the crust of the current city, slowly rising ever upward. I was on the look-out for residue, for texture, for accidents and encounters and unexpected openings. My most meaningful experience with the city was not through its literature, its food or its museums, not even through the soul-scarring affair I carried on in a garret near the Bourse, but through all that walking. Somewhere in the 6th arrondissement I realised I wanted to live in a city for the rest of my life, and specifically, in the city of Paris. It had something to do with the utter, total freedom unleashed from the act of putting one foot in front of the other.

I wore a groove into the Boulevard Montparnasse as I came and went between my flat on the avenue de Saxe and school on the rue de Chevreuse. I learned non-textbook French from the names of the restaurants in between: Les Zazous (named for a kind of jazzy 1940s hepcat in a plaid blazer and a quiff), Restaurant Sud-Ouest & Cie, which taught me the French equivalent of '& Co.', and from a bakery called Pomme de pain I learned the word for 'pine cone', *pomme de pin*, though I never learned why that was a pun worth making. I bought orange juice on the way to class every day at a pretzel shop called Duchesse Anne and wondered who she was and what was her relationship to pretzels. I pondered the distorted French conception of American geography that resulted in a TexMex restaurant called Indiana Café. I walked past all the great cafes lining the boulevard, La Rotonde, Le Sélect, Le Dôme and La Coupole, watering holes to generations of American writers in Paris, whose ghosts hunched under cafe awnings, unimpressed with the way the twentieth century had turned out. I crossed over the rue Vavin, with its eponymous cafe, where all the cool *lycéens* went when they got out of school, assertive cigarette smokers with sleeves too long for their arms, shod in Converse sneakers, boys with dark curls and girls with no make-up.

Soon, emboldened, I wandered off into the streets shooting out from the Jardin de Luxembourg, a few minutes' walk from school. I found myself up near the church of Saint-Sulpice, which was under renovation then, and, like the Tour Saint-Jacques, had been for decades. No one knew if or when the scaffolding around the towers would ever come down. I would sit at the Café de la Mairie on Place Saint-Sulpice and watch the world go by: the skinniest women I'd ever seen wearing linen clothing that would be frumpy in New York but in Paris seemed unreplicably chic, nuns in twos and threes, yuppie mothers who let their small boys wee on tree trunks. I wrote down everything I saw, not knowing yet that the French writer Georges Perec had also sat in that square, in that same cafe, during a week in 1974, and noted the same comings and goings – taxis, buses, people eating pastries, the way the wind was blowing – all in an attempt to get his readers to notice the unexpected beauty of the quotidian, what he called the *infraordinary*: what happens when nothing is happening. I didn't know, either, that *Nightwood*, which would become one of my favourite books, was set at that cafe and in the hotel upstairs. Paris was just beginning to contain – and to generate – all of my most significant intellectual and personal reference points. We had only just met.

As an English major I had wanted to go to London, but thanks to a technicality wound up in Paris instead. Within a month I was transfixed. The streets of Paris had a way of making me stop in my tracks, my heart suspended. They seemed saturated with presence, even if there was no one there but me. These were places where something could happen, or had happened, or both; a feeling I could never have had at home in New York, where life is inflected with the future tense. In Paris I would linger outside, imagining stories to go with streets. In those six months, the streets were transformed from places in between home and wherever I was going into a great passion. I drifted wherever they looked interesting, lured by the sight of a decaying wall, or colourful window boxes, or something intriguing down at the other end, which might be as pedestrian as a perpendicular street. Anything, any detail that suddenly loosened itself, would draw me towards it. Every turn I made was a reminder that the day was mine and I didn't have to be anywhere I didn't want to be. I had an astonishing immunity to responsibility, because I had not ambitions at all beyond doing only that which I found interesting.

I remember when I'd take the metro two stops because I didn't realise how close together everything was, how walkable Paris was. I had to walk around to understand where I was in space, how places related to each other. Some days I'd cover five miles or more, returning home with sore feet and a story or two for my room-mates. I saw things I'd never seen in New York. Beggars (Roma, I was told) who knelt rigidly in the street, heads bowed, holding signs asking for money, some with children, some with dogs; homeless people living in tents, under stairways, under arches. Every quaint Parisian nook had its corresponding misery. I turned off my New York apathy and gave what I could. Learning to see meant not being able to look away; to walk in the streets of Paris was to walk the thin line of fate that divided us from each other.

And then, somehow, by chance, I learned that all that walking around, feeling intensely, constantly moved to scribble what I saw and felt into the floppy notebooks I bought at the Saint-Michel bookstore Gibert Jeune – all that I did instinctively, others had done to such an extent that there was a word for it. I was a *flâneur*.

Or rather – a good student of French, I converted the masculine noun to a feminine one – a *flâneuse*.

Melissa Harrison, *Rain: Four Walks in English Weather* (2016)

The shower cloud blows over, taking its shadow with it across the fields; the sun dazzles briefly off the wet road with its seam of compressed dung, and everything sparkles. April is a good month for leverets, and I know that hares have been seen just outside the village in recent weeks; as I walk I try to tune my eyes to spot their small, brown shapes in the fields on either side . . . If there are any hares around I can't see them; I just hope they're not getting too wet. I decide to take a footpath that runs along the top of a paddock and back to the village. Two comma butterflies dance low over the lush spring grass of the paddock; they spiral, rising and falling, as though describing in the air the structure of their own urgent DNA. Really heavy precipitation can knock butterflies from the air, damaging their wings or leaving them at risk from opportunistic predators, so at the first sign of approaching bad weather they'll tuck themselves away, clinging to the undersides of leaves or creeping into tall grass. But when the shower passes and the sun comes out they're quick to take wing again.

On the distant slopes of the Wrekin the rain has washed the walls of the old quarries, carrying away infinitesimal amounts of minerals from the bare rock faces and minutely weakening the seams in the exposed stone. It's filled the old quarry pits by an amount too small to measure, and in the wooded areas is already being sucked up by the oaks' and ashes' thirsty roots. And across the county and beyond it's fallen on the backs of nesting birds, sitting tight and determined on clutches of blue, or white, or brown, or speckled eggs, or flying back and forth to feed importunate upturned gapes.

A week from now, a dust storm in the Sahara will combine with air pollution to hang over the south-east of the country, eventually to be washed out of the sky by rain and deposited on our car where it's parked in our South London street. But for now it looks as though it's going to be a fine evening in Shropshire, warm and clear, and hopefully a dry Bank Holiday Monday tomorrow. It's good to walk without my hood up so I can hear the blackbirds begin their evening performances; good, too, to note the fresh-washed clarity of the air and the way it carries sound. If I stop walking for a moment I can hear the occasional plinks of the last raindrops falling from the trees by the road.

Helen Mort, 'Kinder Scout', from *No Map Could Show Them* (2016)

Gold light. I wish the day
could break me like an egg

so I'd ooze the same colour, flatten
on the skillet of Mam Tor.

I'd like the summit path to be a knife
that pared me, skin

like apple skin, saving
just my necessary parts.

Surely the best northwesterly
could whip me into lightness,

sugar me, admit the air
so something of this landscape

could be folded in:
September bracken, lichen, stone.

I don't know if I'm ready
to be taken

but I'd like to lie prepared:
unnoticed, important as butter,

softening
on the hill's plate.

Camille T. Dungy, *Guidebook to Relative Strangers: Journeys into Race, Motherhood and History* (2017)

A Good Hike

Outside long enough, I lose the contours of my body and become part of something larger. What I watch for on a good hike are moments of permission, the times my interactions with what is beyond me provide opportunities to know the world in ways different from how I'm used to knowing it. I lose track of my own inhibitions and begin to wonder just what I might be able to do if I allowed myself the full scope of my potential. I become more willing to test my own limits in these circumstances, and I discover the particular freedom that accompanies physical accomplishment coupled with plenty of fresh air in the lungs. A good hike is an exercise in mindfulness, not just racing up and down a hill, but attending to each object passed along the way: the new goose turd on a boulder that suggests a late or aborted migration; the little patches of lichen clumped along the trail looking like discarded blood orange peels slowly drying in late-autumn sun. When I am hiking well, I marvel at everything I see and all I am able to do. A good hike takes me places I haven't been before.

Not all hikes are good hikes. One can race up and down a hill in a state of mindlessness that attends to very little. During the portion of the November afternoon when I fractured my fibula, I wasn't mindfully watching the path. If I had become, at some point earlier on that hike, part of something larger, I returned to an acute consciousness of my individual limits the moment I slipped on wet leaves and caught the toe of my right sneaker on a camouflaged root. The single expletive I shouted was enough to make everyone around me conscious of the contours of my body. I crumpled to the ground, said, 'I just broke my ankle,' and gripped both hands around the site of the injury. If you've ever noticed the way a hurt animal curls around itself, pained and snarling, needing assistance but daring anyone to come near, you have a picture of what I looked like in the Adirondacks that November.

The day had started off on a good foot. The climb up Castle Rock had been simple and gorgeous, a meandering ascent over orange-gold beech leaves, shallow runoff pools, rocks and small boulders. It briefly occurred to me that I should have worn hiking boots, but this was the only hike I was likely to take in the Adirondacks that weekend and it seemed reasonable not to have hauled my bulky boots all the way from California. My running shoes had grip enough, and truly, this was more walk than hike, our pace mitigated by our numbers.

There were twenty-two of us. Our stated goal that weekend was to discuss how to write publishable explorations of the natural world within the ever-more-complicating context of the twenty-first century. One of our number had written a book called *Sick of Nature*, and one had written *The Secret Knowledge of Water*. One would later die in Uganda, presumably of heat exhaustion, while working on a magazine article about walking the length of the Nile. The quietest member of our group was completing a collection of natural history essays called *Things That Are*, and I had just published a poetry anthology called *Black Nature*. Most of the weekend we'd stay in the lodge, talking about writing about nature. This was our chance to walk our talk.

Matthew and Joe, some of the youngest among us, bounded ahead of the pack, Carhartt-clad legs tackling the terrain with ease. When they came to the caves recommended by Suzy, a lodge volunteer and the woman most familiar with the place, they poked around briefly, then, unwilling to be slowed, sought the trail again and seemed to spring upward out of sight.

I'd started out with these two, excited to be outside in new territory. I marked intriguing sights along the way, that goose turd, for instance, and a particularly remarkable stand of naked white beech, but the pace I kept with Matthew and Joe privileged ascent, arrival over journey. I looked, but I certainly didn't linger.

I couldn't keep that pace for long. I was sharing my lungs and body with a nine-week-old fetus, and my will was not the only power my body needed to heed. This was a new state of being for me. Approaching forty, I had never considered having a child before, let alone experienced the physical and often cumbersome realities of what my decision to get pregnant would mean. I'd always set my own schedule. Now waves of nausea tempered my pace. I was trying not to let discomfort slow me, but concern over how my movements jostled my belly took hold and I was reminded, as pregnancy will remind a woman, that my decisions no longer affected me alone.

As I slowed, then stopped briefly, resumed at half pace, then slowed again, most of my fellow hikers passed me. Soon

I found myself walking toward the rear of the pack with the other pregnant lady in our group.

Joni seemed perfectly comfortable taking her time. The path was slippery because of leaf fall and runoff, and she didn't want to chance a tumble. Instead, she stopped periodically and turned full circle, taking in the open blue sky and, below us, Blue Mountain Lake, its dark green water punctuated frequently by small islands and the outcroppings of its ragged shoreline.

Perhaps one day I will be confident and content even while moving slowly. But when we got to the caves, all desire to slow down vanished. The damp, mineral, mossy smell of caves reminds me of my childhood, so when Suzy showed us the passage through, I forgot all inhibitions. I climbed and contorted, grappled and gripped, as if I were a girl again, my center of gravity low and each limb pliable.

Suzy climbed ahead through the first narrow passage, offering the women who followed a hand should they need help. I declined the offer, knowing her small frame was no match for my weight, and aware I could only depend on my own strength and dexterity to pull me up, around, and over the rock face. Despite the fact that my nails had grown hand-model long thanks to my pregnancy, I found holds in the rock. Torquing my knees and ankles, pushing and pulling, and with the thoughtless ease of someone who has been doing a hard task her whole life, I climbed past each of four ever more steep and narrow passages.

Moving through and over rock like that, I come to know it, to feel its sharp points and its forgiving ones, to note what pockets might prove a den for resting creatures and which would safely provide temporary sanctuary for me. Lia, one of the women who moved through the caves behind me, said I'd found holds she'd never have seen. I didn't necessarily see them, either. My body simply knew how to find them. I registered the caves not as a writer, intellectually cataloging the details, but as a dancer, responding physically to what presented itself. I felt like an expert, like the master of Castle Rock. I felt outstanding. I'd forgotten the nausea and bloating of early pregnancy and the trepidation that came along with them, the constant concern over whether I was moving too fast or too slowly or too much or too little for the fetus. I forgot the fetus. I had my lungs all to myself. They were full and my heart was strong.

For the remainder of the ascent I felt good. I felt fit and powerful and happy. I felt like I belonged outside.

The climb down should have been simple. After a short rest at the summit of Castle Rock, where we took pictures of the bright blue lake below us and of our own smiling faces atop the craggy peak, the whole party turned around for the descent. The pre-pregnant me would have been invigorated by the exhilaration of the ascent. I would have felt empowered and ready to take on anything the world threw my way. But I had overextended myself. I was tired before the descent even began, ready to be off the hill and back in the lodge by the fire. I felt pregnant again, weighed down.

I should have taken care with every step, watching for exposed roots, verifying my footing.

I should have exercised Joni's cautious grace. Mindful of my own body and protective of my fetus, I could have paused periodically and examined leaves and lichens.

I should have exerted a little more energy and stuck with the many paddlers who peeled off the trail and kayaked back to the lodge, completing the circuit I'd started that day.

But I did none of this. I was tired and thinking about the car that could cut out the paddling component and drive us more directly back to the lodge. I chatted with my companions about environmental futures, writing conferences, children, students, the recent increase of human/black bear interactions in Colorado. I was walking in a crowd rather than solo or in a group of two or three, as I prefer to hike, and I was behaving as unconsciously as if I were walking through a park in some suburban town. I was just clomping speedily along, poorly calibrated, and inattentive.

And then I broke my ankle.

Kate, the woman I knew best in this group, knelt beside me to assess the damage. Kate had trained as a wilderness first responder. She knew what to do when a person was hurt. She wanted to pull down my sock, to gauge the degree of the swelling, but she could hardly pry my fingers from my leg. 'I need to see it,' she said, looking in my eyes with the reassuringly authoritative gaze of the veterinarian.

'No, you don't,' I said. Trying not to refuse her help, but refusing it nonetheless. 'It's broken. I heard it snap.'

'I heard it, too,' said Lia.

This comforted me just enough that I loosened my grip and let Kate do her work.

Lia had been walking about five feet away when I fell. If she'd heard that sound, a sound more solid and interior than any twig could make, what I thought I'd heard must be true.

The rest of the way off the hill, while the guys insisted it was likely just a very bad sprain, I assured myself I was not some hysterical girl overreacting to a twisted ankle. Kate seemed worried and – I found this sustaining – Lia had heard the bone break.

As a former athlete, I had experience with both joint injuries and broken bones. I'd already undergone two reconstructive surgeries on chronically sprained or dislocated joints. During the preoperative procedures for shoulder surgery over a decade earlier, the anesthesiologist insisted I take a pregnancy test.

'I'm not pregnant,' I assured him.

'Well, I want you to take this test just to be sure.'

'I'm sure I'm not pregnant,' I insisted.

'Please, just take this test. Anesthesia is really bad for babies.'

I took his pee cup, but not before reaffirming my conviction. 'Babies are really bad for Camille,' I said. I believed, then, that having a baby would slow me down, keep me from doing the things I felt were necessary for my happiness.

I remained uninterested in having a child until I met Ray, and then it was less the idea of having a child that convinced me than it was the idea of entering this new phase with *Ray*, my husband, in particular. I wanted to create not so much a baby as *a family*. The adjustments I would have to make in my life seemed more manageable with a quality partner. Still, I was concerned about the repercussions of these necessary adjustments.

Sitting on that pile of November leaves, I worried about what would happen to me and to the fetus if I needed some complicated surgery as a result of this fall. I worried because

I knew that anesthesia is really bad for babies and I'd believed that babies weren't a good idea for a woman like me. I worried that I had been right to worry about how getting pregnant would radically modify all of my decisions.

But these worries were irrelevant. I had to focus on getting off the hill.

We had nearly a mile to walk to the car, and I could bear no weight on my right leg. The first scheme we concocted involved my left side supported by a walking stick harvested off the trail, my right arm wrapped around Drew's shoulder. Six-foot-three, with the build of a man in his late thirties who had played football in high school and who kept himself in decent shape, Drew was the kind of guy you might call if you needed help moving furniture. It seemed obvious that he should be the one to help me.

Unfortunately, though he might have been strong, the one-shoulder arrangement proved inefficient for moving me down the hill. Soon Chip, the next largest in our group, came to help Drew. We discarded the walking stick. The two men now supported me as I hopped slowly forward. As we progressed, the four men in the group rotated positions, Matthew and Joe taking over for Drew and Chip, Drew replacing Matthew, Chip replacing Joe in a round robin game of help haul the crippled girl off the mountain.

I tried to help as much as possible, bounding as high and far forward as I could with each push of my left leg. I lifted my weight with my arms and core so the men did not have to do all the work of hauling me upward and forward. I was self-conscious, wishing I could have been lighter, that I could bear at least a little weight on my right foot. I desperately wanted to get off the mountain as soon as possible, to make myself as light and fast as I could.

I am a big-boned girl – 'Thick in all the right places,' my husband would say – and I didn't want to be a burden on the men who helped haul me down the hill. More important, I didn't want to appear helpless. I could play the damsel in distress by letting them be gentlemen who lent me their handkerchiefs and opened my car doors, but I weighed as much or more than most of them, and I was used to taking care of myself. The version of gender roles that rests on a woman's daintiness and readiness to be rescued broke down with me. I think of Sojourner Truth's 'Ain't I a Woman?' speech, delivered over a hundred and fifty years ago and still reminding us that the image of women as meek and dainty was a picture of white women. Black women, to borrow Zora Neale Hurston's early twentieth-century phrase, have long been treated as the mules of the world.

I have a friend, another African American woman, who is over six feet tall in heels and has the well-proportioned body to accommodate that long frame. She's a big girl, but not fat. When the issue of body mass index comes up, she's likely to fly into a rage. The standard BMI does not take into account muscle mass, bone density, or other, often ethnically related, considerations that might elevate a woman's count. There are several problems with this. One is that otherwise fit women who carry a heftier muscle mass on a thicker frame could easily feel pathological even in bodies that, with appropriate adjustments to the scale, would be well within a normal range. Another dangerous side effect is that women who actually are far too heavy ignore BMI charts and other scales since even at weights that are healthy for their bodies these standards label them overweight. My friend was denied life insurance because a doctor, basing his assessment on the body mass index alone, wrote *obese* in her medical records. I've seen her run her finger across a BMI chart, read where she is positioned despite the fact she wears a perfectly reasonable size twelve dress on her five-foot-nine body, and remind anyone who will listen that for the sake of higher profits in her ancestral past, she was bred to be this big.

Most of my life, my way of dealing with the feeling that my body was outsized or out of place has been to make sure I excel at whatever I ask my body to do. If I could hike as fast, climb with as much agility, ski as competently, paddle as aggressively as the folks around me, I assumed no one would think twice about the fact that a relatively big black girl was on the mountain, lake, or trail. Outside, people only care about size if it slows them down. I tried never to be the one to slow anyone down. This pregnancy, this injury, these put my pride at the mercy of much that was beyond me, and I have a deep aversion to being at the mercy of things that are beyond my control.

The men were all at least three inches taller than I am, and Drew nearly nine, so my abdomen and upper body stretched to accommodate their shoulders as I lifted and pulled myself along the trail. I could sense the protestations of my fetus with every hop and, more than once, I had to wonder how long it would be until I could make use of a bathroom. But my left leg would land, and the men would be ready, immediately, to take another stride, so I coiled my energy and worked to spring myself forward again. This jostled the offending ankle, splinted only by Drew's handkerchief, which Kate had wrapped around the injury site and the bottom of my running shoe.

As a five-legged cluster, we often came upon boggy points in the path. At first we tried to hop around them, worrying they'd be too slippery, but eventually we trudged straight through, trying to move as directly as possible. Kate or Lia walked ahead, telling us where the trail grew tricky and suggesting how we might proceed. We'd come to wet or rocky patches and I hopped, with the help of my companions, from one rock to another eighteen inches away. The men grew tired, I was beyond exhausted, and we'd hardly moved two-tenths of a mile.

Everyone wanted to be off the mountain, and since the two-shoulder carry wasn't progressing us as efficiently as we would like, Drew suggested he carry me on his back. No one had offered me a piggyback ride since my father, when I was about eight years old, told me I was too big for such nonsense. Still, what would seem illogical under normal circumstances now sounded like an option worth exploring. He squatted, and with the help of four hands, I used my tiring left leg to hop onto his back.

Drew carried me this way as far as he could. Because I had difficulty gripping with only one leg, the women followed behind, supporting my butt. 'You didn't think you'd get a butt massage as part of this bargain, did you?' asked Kate.

'Well, I was hoping at least one good thing could happen today,' I replied.

Often during this ordeal, I engaged in bouts of magical thinking in which I made no observations but those that increased the hilarity of the situation. I suppose this was my way of recalibrating the scale, focusing on what would get me through to the next moment rather than dwelling on how difficult and painful my predicament was.

Adrenaline, and my insistence on noting all possible hilarity, stocked me full of laughter. I became a best-case-scenario spinner. The fracture could have happened farther up the mountain, on the steep and boulder-laden part of the trail. I might have done this on one of my solo hikes. Then how would I have gotten off the hill? Each time Drew stripped off an article of clothing or one of his outdoorsman accessories, I joked that he was just looking for an excuse to run naked through the woods. I teased Kate each time she braved a peek at my ankle despite the knowledge I'd grown feral in my protection of the joint. I joked about my fetus and how, when it was born healthy and whole, I would play with its little arms and legs, and tell the baby I was glad its skeleton was strong, since the calcium for those bones was borrowed from Mama's. I knew my fetus's skeletal development, though coincident with my injury, had nothing to do with my fracture, but it was a pleasant way to involve my unborn child in our adventure.

People often talk about the survival mechanisms of fat kids, the way we frequently perfect the role of being the funniest student in class. We want to make sure people laugh with us rather than at us. The ego's bruised a little less that way. Though I started out the hike at the head of the pack, proving I was able to keep up with the spriest among us, the realities of my new, enlarged body slowed me, and now this fracture had stopped me entirely. I'd transformed from the fit master of Castle Rock into a heavy, useless burden. I felt awful needing the men to carry me. But instinct, brought on by history and adrenaline, told me that if I couldn't make myself useful, at least I could make us all laugh.

There was still a long trail ahead, and laughter was a better alternative than yelling or crying.

We moved forward in this manner maybe fifty yards. Seventy? Then it was back to the two-shoulder hobble. Then the piggy-back again, before which Drew removed his birding binoculars, his glasses. Each time I climbed on his back, he walked as far as he could, then we returned to the two-shoulder hobble, letting two of the other men spell Drew as he wiped the sweat from his neck and forehead.

I couldn't tell you how long we kept at it. The men's speed picked up, which would have been a good thing, but for the fact that this sent my leg jostling to such a degree I had to beg them to stop.

Then I came up with the perfect solution.

I collapsed to my hands and knees and moved forward of my own volition. No more jostling ankle. Sweet relief.

'You're going to crawl?' asked Matthew.

'This is going to work. You guys have carried me far enough. I can do the rest on my own. Look, I'm moving pretty quickly.'

For a short while no one said a thing. I was clearly set on this solution. I'd left no room for argument, and, it was true, I was moving at a clip that exceeded what we'd managed thus far.

The sun was positioned at the angle where it rests just before it races toward the horizon. All of us knew we didn't have much time before dark.

Forward I crawled.

Chip – the man who had proposed this trip in the first place, the man who wanted to see what the new generation of American environmentalist writers valued most and so invited a group of relatively young nature writers to the Adirondacks for a confab about the future of the genre – Chip looked on at my progress with speechless horror.

He told me later he was terrified some other group of hikers would come along and discover all these white people standing around watching a black girl crawl through the woods.

Chip wasn't entirely off base in his assessment of the situation. Part of why we treat people horribly, why we might make the one subjugated other among us crawl while the rest walk through the woods, why we damage people's bodies, or ridicule them, why we work to break people down, is because we want another human being to give body and will over to us so we can do with it what we desire. Pain, embarrassment, hopelessness, fear: a combination of these can erase pride from a human spirit in short order. Once pride is absent, control is that much easier to command.

Those of us who are conscious of human history know the pervasiveness with which one person's will has been pressed on another's. And as environmentalists, we were all well aware of the ease with which people set up distinctions between themselves and anything they choose to categorize as separate from, and therefore subject to, themselves. What Chip feared was that some outsider would look at our party and assume that a play of dominance was under way. He was afraid it would look as if he were the one working to subjugate me.

Chip was silent on the mountain because his concern about the appearance of oppression was so great. Yet he was able to describe his reaction at breakfast, laughing while he did so, because by the next day the concern felt humorous, no longer a real threat.

The whole time we were working to get me off the mountain, I thought I was worried about the pain in my ankle and the burden of my weight. I realize now that my other big worry, what I feared the whole time on the hill, was that I would have to let go of my pride.

These are the ways human history cross-pollinates with all our interactions in the world. Had Joe, with his Carhartts and Jesus haircut, his Montana roots, his wife and infant child back in northern Iowa, been the one to break his ankle, this essay might have gone in a completely different direction. Or Matthew, the urban homesteader who traveled across the world visiting lithium mines in Bolivia and garbage dumps in the Philippines, then returned to Brooklyn to write articles for *Harper's*. What direction would this essay have taken had he been the one transported a mile off the hill? What about Amy, so fine-boned Drew could surely have draped her over one shoulder and sprinted with her to the car? What gendered nuances would this essay take on had she been the injured party? And what racial nuances, Amy being a white woman from Texas, Drew a black man from South Carolina? What do I do with the knowledge that the man I was most able to give my body over to happened to be the one other black person in our group? What if the essay were written from

Drew's perspective? The largest and strongest and blackest among us, he was the one who put in the hardest physical labor. Try as I might to lose myself to something larger, I'm always reminded of the boundaries of the body: we are bound by gender; we are bound by appearance; we are bound by race. These are ways human history cross-pollinates all my interactions.

As I was crawling along the dirt path, though, I wasn't fretting about the ways history repeats itself. I wasn't worrying about the suffering the world and I might cause my child. For this brief time, I wasn't troubled by nausea or the pain around my belly. I was just crawling.

Matthew stood above me. 'You can't crawl,' he said.

'Why not? It seems to be working just fine.'

'You'll destroy your hands and knees. Get up. We won't let you do that to yourself.' As Matthew spoke, the other men, who seemed to have been frozen by my insistence but who heard in Matthew's words a distillation of their thought, sprang into action again, gripped my arms, and pulled me into a standing position.

Forced to my feet by the men, but loath to resume the uterus-stretching, ankle-jostling, pride-crushing shoulder haul, I asked for two of the walking sticks people had gathered as we progressed. For the course of perhaps four steps, I tried to crutch myself along.

The sun was beginning its rapid slide toward the horizon, and Chip would have none of my walking on my own. So the uterus-stretching, ankle-jostling, pride-crushing shoulder haul resumed.

If we were to get off the mountain before the darkness caught us entirely, I would have to give myself over to these men.

I said, so quietly I'm not sure anyone heard me over their panting, 'Let go and let gods.'

I was being facetious.

I was completely earnest.

I stopped working to lighten their load, an effort that may well have been complicating matters. I revealed the full weight of my body and let the men bear it as far and as quickly as they could. I had to let them take me, and to do this I had to let go of any pretense of pride and control.

The group of people on whom I found myself dependent were relative strangers. And yet, as I was at their mercy in the wild, this was the best group I could imagine falling among. Kate, with her first responder training, kept an eye on my leg and my face, warning the men to slow down if I started to look too ashen. Chip kept a clear gauge on the sun, remaining realistic about how much light we had left and making sure our forward pace kept steady. Lia, who'd heard my bone crack and didn't want me to be jostled any more than necessary, watched our path, guiding us so we could concentrate on smooth forward transitions.

When I asked Drew later if his upper body wasn't sore (by the end of the weekend mine burned from the effort to lift myself as I draped my arms around the men's high shoulders), he said he was actually pleased to discover his exercise regimen seemed to be working. He'd developed what he thought of as a practical workout, training his body to be useful in circumstances such as the one we'd encountered.

I found myself thinking about the urban students I taught at San Francisco State University, in whom I tried to instill an appreciation of the wonders of nature. Many of them were incredulous, even scared. They worried about what might happen to them out there. Mountain lions, rapists, and bears, oh my. I worried about taking my story back to them. What kind of advertisement would I make crutching into the classroom after a weekend of hiking? But I realized that the key to the story was the company I'd found myself among. These turned out to be people I could trust with my body, people who would find a way to get me off the mountain and get me the help I needed. Rather than telling a tale of fear and devastation, I could talk to my students about how affirming this experience turned out to be. I was scared, certainly, but through the journey I discovered I hadn't needed to be.

Kate Davis, 'She teaches herself to walk across a limestone landscape', from *The Girl Who Forgets How to Walk* (2018)

Start
check
step
check
step
slope
slip stop
stop stop stop

Start
step
step step
slope check stop

Start
check
step
check
step
slip
slip stop

Start
step
check
step
slope
step
check
step
step
step
step step stomp

Start step
check step
step step
step step
step step step step step

Katherine May, *The Electricity of Every Living Thing: A Woman's Walk in the Wild to Find Her Way Home* (2018)

I am walking, now, as a kind of compulsion. I keep my week-ends free for it, giving noncommittal answers when friends suggest we should get together. In the new dawn of AS, I want to find out what not getting together feels like. I'm sick of people. I suspect people are making me sick. I want to be alone, in the January drear, with the voluminous space of the countryside around me, even if it is spiked with blackthorn and bare branches.

Bert has a friend over to play today, a friend from nursery. I made arrangements myself with the other mother in the cloakroom, as the two boys pretended to put on their shoes. We have exchanged friendly texts, in which it has been made politely clear that she will not leave her child alone with us, but that she will stay. I know better than to take this personally; everybody stays these days. I suppose we all have to endlessly suspect each other of one perversion or another, as though the world is populated entirely by latent Jimmy Saviles, waiting to spring on our children. Those of us who lack this anxiety probably stay anyway, drinking tea and making awkward conversation, because we don't want to look like we don't care. And so we all take it in turns to invade each other's space while we could be doing something useful like tidying the house or having lunch with our partners, but we don't dare to argue because that would send out the signal that we have better things to do than constantly fawn over our children.

Anyway. In the days running up to the child's visit, it becomes clear to me that (a) I ought to be the one who entertains this mother, not H; and (b) that I have such a pronounced aversion to doing so that it's keeping me awake at night. How long do these playdates last? Two hours? Three? What on earth am I supposed to say to her in that time? A lifetime of being told I'm offhand and unfriendly forces me to say, at this point, that she seems very nice. But that doesn't make the enforced socialisation any more of an appetising prospect.

On Saturday morning, I cave in and ask H if he'll do the honours while I go walking.

'Of course,' he says. 'I never thought you'd stay anyway.'

'But I ought to,' I say. 'We all know I ought to.'

'Who says?'

'Everyone. Society. Mumsnet. I don't know. We're supposed to have coffee and "natter" about . . . whatever women talk about. Our children, I should think.'

'Oh well,' says H. 'I'll manage.'

'Just don't tell her I'm walking. Tell her I'm working.'

'Why?'

'Walking's a leisure activity. I'm not supposed to avoid her for something like that.'

It doesn't feel like a leisure activity, though; it feels like survival. I drive myself back to Chartham, park by the level crossing, and cross back over the main road. I have to walk all the way back up to the top of the lane (and past a sign that warns of walkers in the road) before I find the turning I should have taken last week, discreetly tucked into a driveway, but nevertheless perfectly well signposted and obvious on the map.

I walk through farmland, under a railway bridge, and then past a set of sorry-looking caravans that probably host itinerant pickers in warmer seasons. I am back in an orchard, but this one is enormous, set on a slope and divided into fields. The trees here are chest-height and don't have branches so much as tangles of wiry twigs that wisp around them. They represent some kind of calculation, I suspect, that balances how many apples they can carry against how easily reached the fruit might be. I'm sure this calculation has something to do with the piles of bright red apples at the base of every trunk, even after all the leaves have gone. They glow against the low-sun gloom, an absurd, unwanted glut.

The map shows that I cut through the middle of this orchard to make my way into Old Wives Lees, but I cannot find a waymarked path. After stalking the edge of the field for a while, I decide just to walk between the lines of trees. The ground beneath my feet crunches with ice. I can see the general direction in which I need to go, but this off-roading panics me slightly anyway. What are the rules, I wonder, about trespassing on farmland? It suddenly occurs to me that the reason I feel so at home on the South West Coast Path is because it's almost impossible to get lost with the sea at your right. If nothing else, it is at least always clear which way is north. Here, far inland, I have no way of navigating. At this time of year, in the middle of the day, I have no idea whether the sun is even rising or setting.

There comes a point, I suppose, when every walker needs to buy a compass. But I'd choose getting lost like this any day over getting lost in the maze of small talk. Sometimes, getting lost is a pleasurable alternative.

Raynor Winn, *The Salt Path* (2018)

We were well into our second day of the fudge diet and it wasn't going well. Headaches, dizziness and hunger were now constant. We could have diverted inland to a café in Morwenstow, but that would have used unknown amounts of money that we barely had, and when you start a diet it's best to stick to it. We'd be in Bude later anyway.

A mile further on and we knew we'd been stupid. We should have gone back and refilled the water bottles, but we couldn't bear to retrace our steps and so kept moving forwards. The heat was intense on the open cliff top, bouncing back from the scorched earth and reflecting from the blue sea. Not a breath of wind, just heat wrapping around in a hot, dusty, sweaty, suffocating fog. Then we drank the last drop of water. The heat pressed us down; it took every ounce of willpower to stay on our feet and keep moving. Where there should have been streams, there were only dried-up cracks in the earth. The thirst overtook the hunger in a primal craving for water: we needed it and we needed it now.

Stupid, stupid, stupid.

Stupid to think we could walk this path, to not have enough money, to pretend we weren't homeless, to get the court procedure wrong, to lose the children's home, to not have enough water, to pretend we weren't dying, to not have enough water.

Stupid, stupid, stupid.

Nancy Gaffield, *Meridian* (2019)

Lewes to East Grinstead

*– They would, she thought, going on again, however long
they lived, come back to this night . . .*
Virginia Woolf, *To the Lighthouse*

we are all connected
    all experiences
        are along a continuum

What is a line
a length
without breadth
    the trace of
        a moving point
    a procedure

            light
            framed in astragals

everyone wants to
die at home
    I'm inside
        that train whistle
    sickness for / of

I don't know how
to go there

            – in the fragrant pines
           and the cedars dusk and dim

I only know walking
is involved in it.

The geese pass in high skeins
    autumn is coming

I am six years old again
    learning to read
        the landscape

making my way by sight by history
    by the compass
        by luck

imagining the lines of longitude
    as twin ropes
        of a swing

in the left hand is Sussex
    in the right is the 105th Meridian West
        UTC-7:00 Mountain Time North

the Prospect Road interchange
    in Fort Collins aligns
        almost precisely along it

it also passes through
    Union Station
        in Denver

        – I wander thro' each charter'd street
      mountain towns
        (Stout, COLO Pop. 47½)

Don't look back
    or you will plunge
        into terrae incognitae

night terrors
    devoid
        of any coordinates

the haggard dawn pulls
    you from your bed
        it's time to go
    a-wanderin

The face on the barroom floor in
actual fact belonged to Edna 'Nita'
Davis, 1936. Gold from Central
City, a red-dirt town, the richest
square mile on earth. Here was the
lure of the foreign back in your
own back yard.

I cut myself free
  adrift now
    in the outer limits

This is a tale of two continents.

An observant solitary woman
  strolls the South Downs Way
she is no armchair traveller
  but a non-paying customer
in a commercial world
  walking along at crab pace
sometimes sideways
  crossing the pond
she steps into the water
  her pockets brimming
    with the eyes of the dead

How far we have come to go home again.

Coming into woods now
following scent trails
vapour trails

counting steps & channelling
Grandma Hazard
our simian arms

swinging at the elbow
that final flick
of the wrist

I walk with empty hands
amongst the nut-gatherers
tracking an impression

after those that made it
have passed by
presence in absence

I walk through dappled wood
where the nut-gatherers
course

yellow leaf-fall
snake casings
parasols and other fungi

knots fold into gnarls
     lines of genealogy
        kinship

twilight flickers through
     gaps in the trees
        a path of light

Kathleen Jamie, *Surfacing* (2019)

You are not lost. You followed your map. There is a path — there is always a path through the wood; there has been since the dawn of time. The trees step aside to make one. It's a ghost trail, an animal trail maybe for deer or badgers. There are no animals, it's daytime. No wolves for sure and no bears.

You sense the woods miss the bears; they ought to be here huffing around the old trunks and berry-shrubs, but there's no huffing now. Wolves, though — the wood is old enough to remember them, just.

But you're standing in the wood, stock-still and listening and your hearing has sharpened. There fall the tiny tin-tack calls of birds foraging in the treetops, the race of water in a burn.

And now there is a moth. She appears fluttering in front of you. If this was a fairy tale she might want you to follow her, but she passes and will flatten her grey wings against the grey trunk of a tree. She has never been seen before and never will again, that was it — her sole appearance in our human world, and now it's done.

What are you doing here anyway, in the woods? Ah, well, that is the question. You wanted to think about all the horror.

The everyday news – the guns, the wars, the children's tears down ashy faces, the chainsaws, the sea creatures tangled in plastic . . .

No, not think about it exactly but consider what to do with the weight of it all, the knowing . . . how to cope with it scroll down flick the page unplug the telly send a few quid. Really? Or take a long walk in the wood 'cause you are the lucky one and can do that, you can just shut up shop and go let the wood embrace you.

And here you are.

Sasha Dugdale, 'The Fall of the Rebel Angels', from *Deformations* (2020)

They didn't fall. It wasn't a pillar of legs and arms
a downpour of limbs, a shaft of flesh
like a rainstorm, dark over the sea –

No, they walked. They shouldered packs
laced boots, adjusted straps.
In hi-spec technical wear,
fleeces, gaiters, fearless, the angels
dropped from mountain top
and picked through the debris of rock
hopped over pavements, sundew, grikes
down scarps and slopes
entering the world on the thinnest paths,
the GRs from the stars
the trails, the aura
of a rope team on a glacier
the scramble, the clumsy jump
the odd angel on a bog,
jumping like a man from clump to clump
of cottongrass, falling into mud,
on a seraphic arse, over stiles and gates

and shifting slate in drystone walls,
built before the world knew how to fall,
and bathing in tarns, marvelling at
lambs, napping under pines
walking, walking in angelic lines.

And when they slept their up-till-then
unused legs kept walking in their sleep, their dreams were
of rights-of-way. And even when the coming of
day meant binding feet and the dampness of wings
still they hoisted their packs and took their flasks
and walked and walked, lacing the land
with endless small tracks, which led
(where angels did not fear to tread)
down into valleys and snaking over passes
shining tracks, visible to the naked
eye, the man in glasses, the woman
holding a map. Daily trespassing
angels, angels who walked, and fell
from grace into mountain streams
forgive us our lack
of dreams, we have forgotten
how to rebel.

Anita Sethi, *I Belong Here: A Journey Along the Backbone of Britain* (2021)

Walking as a Woman of Colour

Soon I see another sign for the Pennine Way and am stepping out into open fields, the village quickly falling away to leave countryside completely empty of any human. I will now be walking 15 kilometres uphill through this landscape to reach Malham, following paths, tracks and that strong river, and also navigating areas where there are not such well-worn paths at all. As I walk up the valley, what is supposed to be a gentle section of the Way, I am already feeling the strain, a night of sleeplessness not helping. Despite having brought the bare minimum of belongings, soon pain spreads seemingly to my very backbone. I think of creatures who carry their homes on their backs – turtles, tortoises, crabs, snails – and wish I could bear mine with such ease. My companion assures me I will get used to the weight, that my stamina will increase. I want to walk upwards, to rise through the Pennines, but there is physical and emotional pain involved in pushing past your limits. Every footstep feels arduous.

My companion asks me how it feels to be a woman of colour walking through such a village as the one earlier where I stuck out like a sore brown thumb – the differences between our skin colours seemed pronounced. But I tell him I don't want to talk, that every calorie of energy needs to go into walking. As my shoulders strain, I wonder if I will end up writing How Not to Walk the Pennine Way, but then the uphill section flattens out into meadowland, filling my field of vision, a sheer beauty of greenness, many shades from the dark copse to the luminous grass, the brightest green I have seen.

I walk deeper into the openness and it seems to embrace me. Then we stop for a breather and I lay down my bag and savour the weight off my shoulders. I stretch out my arms and feel my muscles relax and the hurt lessen in intensity. This is why it is worth it, for this wonderful sense of the world opening out. I breath in and the fresh smell of grass fills me, so potent it is almost as if I can taste it too.

Above all I love looking at the grass, which stretches like a green skin over the surface of the earth, covering whatever lies within its body. It is easy here, surrounded by the glorious green skin of the earth, to become blissfully oblivious of my own skin, unlike while walking through the village, unlike while walking through so much of the world.

Polly Atkin, 'Unwalking', from *Much With Body* (2021)

We cannot set out too early no never – even late
    morning no
– not out – not in the mornings when our enemy
    gravity is the most
possible baggage and the world indecipherable the body
    its own
most possible baggage – property quite impossible to
    refuse – to simply
walk away from. This is not triviality.
It is violence to say to walk is human.

Refusal is our greatest blessing. Lightness is not
    a choice.

If I seem to you to be travelling light
it is because the infinite mass of my body
is non-apparent to the untrained observer.
The dead planet of me. By the time I am visible
    on earth
I will be nothing but dust and soundless echo.

To walk is not humane. Simply. It is not getting.
   Always, everywhere,
people have not walked, veining the earth with
   unpaths, unlines
of desire, so you have called them invisible. No
   footsteps. Others
– striked out – entirely ourselves – implying –
   to be consumed.

There are destinations without journeys, things you will
   never see if you
walk walk walk walk walk

Waiting is not the opposite of walking.
Unwalking is not the same as waiting.
I do not have to move to be moved. Are you moved?

The body is what I cannot untake with me what
   I cannot
leave behind what I cannot not discover, continually,
   along the way,
what I cannot undiscover, unhook myself from,
   slip my arms out from
like a rucksack, old baggage, old body, bag of rocks
   I carry with me.
My everything. What cannot be lost, on a walk
   an unwalk a wait or ever.

Two roads diverged in a yellow wood
And neither of them were accessible.

Two roads diverged in a wood and I –
I couldn't travel either of them.

The future is accessible: the most distant place
on an inaccessible road. With every step it seems
    to move further
and every step hurts. What is a sensible shoe to
    a sensible body?

I am all sensibility. I feel keenly. To walk is a risk
    and my relationship
to risk is fractious. I unwalk. I am very sensible.

Last time I was told to bring comfortable shoes
I replied 'there are no comfortable shoes
unless you can bring me a comfortable body.'
No one offered me a comfortable body.

This is what I learnt in the course of unwalking.
When I spend a day I feel exhausted – so I pace –
    a quality
of attention which is an excellent thing.

Every dislocation is equally important or unimportant,
    the joints
turning wrong, doubling back in the most lonely places.

Unlovely, undemocratic, unreasonable.
The line of unwalking is persistent self-interest.

We must become experts if the body is to articulate
    itself, not
dearticulate itself. This is not so much unromantic
    as reasonable.
Knees, hips, ankles, wrists are natural halting places.
Walking is not so much romantic as unreasonable,
    the flavour
of walking too rare and too extraordinary.

Any walk an expedition when to unwalk is quite
    ordinary, unexceptional,
just what we do, daily, unwalking in all weathers
    every season of the body,
unwalking a continuum upon which the least emphatic
occurrences are registered clearly.

Any stickman, through long use, will adjust itself
    to the pain.
(If you're fit to walk they'll declare you fit to work)

There are so many ways through a landscape we cannot
    choose.
The project of an unwalk will be to remain adequate.
One continues through effort of will not fidelity –
    there is no fidelity –
there is no natural span. This is what we have survived.

    We who unwalk are not without value.
    We are not without value. We are not without.

This is the largest experience we can have.

There are walks on which I lose myself, become
two places.
There are walks on which I lose.

The horizon grows wider, the hills gather round.
They will not return me, to myself, or at all.

Merryn Glover, *Of Stone and Sky* (2021)

But the happiest times and the best stories were out walking. Life on the farm was so relentless there was little opportunity, but whenever she could, she stole away with us. It was partly her Traveller blood, but also the need (never spoken but shared by us all) to be away from Gid. Sometimes she only had an hour to slip off to the Green Bothy where she gathered wild garlic and mushrooms in the woods as we splashed and swam. Sometimes a whole sweet afternoon to take a jammy piece up An Sgiath where she always laid her hands on three of the stones. Sometimes, very rarely, an overnight.

On the longer trips we nearly always went with the MacPhersons, the Munros' nearest neighbours and dearest friends, though Gid always made excuses about the sheep and never came. Their son, Fachie, our shinty team goalie and a keen shot on his air rifle, was Colvin's best buddy (after me, of course, though everyone thought of me as his sister). Margaret – Mrs Mac to us – was short and tubby, surprisingly fit and a legendary baker, while Dougie – Mr Mac – could name every tree and flower, bird and beast. He bored us with his elegies for the lost forests and the devastated land, and it was years before I learned to pay attention, but back then he just smiled sadly and shook his head as we interrupted him or scampered off.

Both he and Agnes loved the Cairngorms, and though he was often in their lower reaches for his forestry work, she could rarely do more than gaze at them across the valley. The year Colvin, Fachie and I were nine, they took us for a longer walk than we had ever ventured before. *Higher up and deeper in!* was Mr Mac's rallying cry as the maps were spread across the table at Shepherd's Cottage. It was September, and we set off early in the cold dark, bundling into the MacPherson's Land Rover in our coats and hats, squished in beside canvas rucksacks and their dog who panted hot breath on our knees. We drove through a thick pool of mist, over the bridge and on to Glenmore forest where we started walking in the grey dawn. The woods smelled of damp earth and pine, the ferns spread with cobwebs in lacy pavilions. We steadily gained height through the cloud, the path getting steeper, the trees thinner and our chatter falling away as our packs grew heavy and our breath short. Mr Mac told stories of the wartime foresters who came from Norway, Labrador and Newfoundland, those who had married and stayed, and those who still wrote to him. Agnes told stories of the Green Fairy Dogs and the Raven's Stone and the Old Grey Man of Ben MacDui. Mrs Mac just chuckled and passed round the shortbread.

And then, without warning, we stepped above the cloud and into sun. I'd never seen the like of it before – the great white sea filling the strath below while we stood on a height of glory. We whooped and laughed and cast off our packs, startling a hare and causing a herd of deer to lift their heads. Joy was our companion for that walk, up, up into the corries and high passes, the wind-blown ridges and the summits of stone and sky. At rushy burns where dragonflies hovered, we drank the clear cold water and, stopping for lunch, gathered the last of the wild berries and skipped stones across a shining loch. Higher up, we saw dotterel scampering so close they made us laugh and a raven pass overhead with a dark croak. We knew we had wandered into the plains of heaven and would never want to leave.

Sarah Moss, *The Fell* (2021)

Kate is out and moving, going somewhere, the hill rising under
her feet and the sky ahead of her. Wind in the trees and her
body working at last, climbing, muscle and bone doing what
they're made for. She won't be long, really she won't, only a
sip of outside, fast up the lane and over the fields, just a little
way up the stone path for a quick greeting to the fells. She'll
come near no one; there won't be hikers out here now, barely
an hour of daylight left, nothing in the weather to call folk
onto the hills. There's only Breck End up the lane and she
won't even follow the path up the side of the farmyard, she'll
walk wide over the field, not chat to Jill's horses the way she
usually does, because if mink can catch it from people, why
not horses, don't they say the first common cold came from
a horse but this one goes the other way, cats and dogs catch-
ing it from their owners. Colour is fading from the moor
ahead, but the chestnut tree by the wall is full of starlings in
loud conversation and the bumps of next year's buds already
swelling on the branches. Normally she'd pause to admire the
starlings – so pretty, their speckles and their iridescence – but
she's not wasting this stolen time pausing, there's plenty of
pausing going on indoors all over Europe. She strides on, feels

the grip of boots on tarmac, the dullness of wet leaves. There's grass down the middle of this road, still poking green through the mud, and brimming potholes reflecting the bare branches overhead. Damp, not quite raining. Keep moving, get warm. The relief of it, being out, being alone, starting to warm up from her own effort, wind and sky in her lungs, raindrops on her face, weather. There'll be a scarf and extra mittens in the backpack, probably, she usually keeps them there, it's always easier to get out of the door if the bag's already packed, but best save them for the higher ground, good to have something else to put on above the treeline. The beat of her feet, the beat of her heart, pick up.

The lights are already on at Breck End, and from the track she can see Jill moving around the kitchen, one of the kids blue in the light of a screen upstairs. Off school again, must be. And there's Neil going into the barn, Kate's about to call and wave when she remembers, presses herself instead into the deepening shadow of the hedge. It's like skiving school, she thinks, the way they used to try to sneak down the drive to the shops for sweets and crisps, crouching and dashing from bush to bush. She's an outlaw. She pulls her hood forward over her face, waits until Neil's gone to climb the stile. Will Jill recognise her if she looks up and sees someone crossing the field? Best just go fast, not that Jill would – but you can't tell, any more, who will understand, it's surprising who turns out to think going outside at all is unnecessary and it's ridiculous, everyone knows indoor transmission is the problem, if the people in charge had any sense they'd be setting limits on how many hours you can spend inside, shooing people out into the wind and the fresh air instead of locking us in. When did we become a species whose default state is shut up indoors? Earlier for women than men, probably, men always setting things up to have the best bits themselves, though Matt would say war and street violence and he's not wrong, the girls are walking the boys home these days, less likely to get stabbed with girls around. Were walking the boys home. When they went out in the first place. Has knife crime dropped, and if so, by more than domestic violence has risen? We're a living experiment, she thinks, in the intensive farming of humans, which is another silly overstatement, no one's force-feeding us antibiotics or cutting bits off us so we can't run away and it's all in the name of safety, not profit. Well, mostly, give or take – Whisht, whisht. Look at the sheep, safely grazing. Look at the dry-stone walls, some of which probably stood through the Spanish Flu and even the Black Death. Look at the oak, twisted and bony, the last tree before she crosses the stone footbridge and the moor rises up under the sky. Listen to the wind over the heather.

Dusk is slow this time of year. She still has a little while. She should make it at least up to the col, to where the old stone packhorse route crosses the hill and you can see across the high plateau towards the city below. She's seen photos of the city now, quiet on a weekday lunchtime as it used to be – well, never, really, not since they ended the Sunday closing. There's no point in thinking about how this will ever end. All the other plagues ended, sooner or later, though most of them went away as well as coming back, some years, some decades, better than others, and people lived and loved and built houses and planted trees and made food and clothes and – and stained glass, travelled, even, made music and put on plays. Ring a ring o' roses. Smallpox, typhoid, cholera: probably more people have lived through epidemics than not over the last few centuries. And of course life won't go back to the way it was, it never does and rarely should. There will be holes in the children's education, a generation that's forgotten or never learnt how to go to a party, people of all ages who won't forget to be afraid to leave the house, to be afraid of other people, afraid to touch or dance or sing, to travel, to try on clothes – whisht, she thinks again, hush now. Walk.

Sonia Overall, *Heavy Time* (2021)

To Ely & Walsingham

Walking into the city is walking into chaos. London Bridge. Cheapside. A tangle of weaving feet, bus fumes, cigarette smoke, irritation.

This is the beginning of pilgrimage leg two, cutting a long north-east line through Hertfordshire and Cambridgeshire to Ely. The rest of today will get me across London; beyond that, I've a long way to go.

The fire on the soles of my feet rekindles. I stop at a chemist for another hit of blister plasters and buy a couple of protein bars. It's only now that I realise how little I have been eating compared to a day at work or home. I'm burning the calories, but there are no regular meals.

I've not done this since early student days. It's hedonistic, but with a hint of the pilgrim's fast or the hermit's asceticism. There is unexpected freedom in this abstinence, of eating when hungry and not by the clock, or by times fixed by the appetites or schedules of others. Skipping meals is antisocial; eating together a form of ritual, a bonding, a needful element of family. Sharing a table at the end of a day or talking shop over a lunchtime sandwich are social contracts. Communal meals remind us of common ground and collective concerns. The problem is squeezing these moments into the routines of work and school, chores and sleep. We eat at our desks. We cram rather than savour. I must overeat all the time, the kind of publicly-enforced overeating that is negligible on a day-to-day basis. It's hard to imagine returning to that pattern of socially-induced self-harm, but I will do, soon, gradually reneging into bad habits, bending the body's needs to those of others, swallowing another little bit of self-will.

Food and flesh. I pass the Golden Boy of Pye Corner. I'm heading to Smithfield and St Bartholomew the Great, two sites of burnings: the reach of the Great Fire, the pyres of faith and obstinacy. The choice of saint feels apt, given that Bartholomew is often depicted holding his own skin, flayed and ready for the griddle. There's the smell of roasting, the sound of drilling, burnt afternoon odours drifting from the dark innards of the Butcher's Hook and Cleaver. The bar next door has steak and brisket on the menu, a smog of sacrificial grease in the air.

I want to admire the well-preserved Tudor Gatehouse of St Barts, but for all its architectural interest I find it sinister and oppressive, the portal to a dark past. This is slaughterhouse territory, a space steeped in the sounds and smells of despair: humiliation, grief, rage, roaring approval, roaring disapproval, bellowing animals. The buildings themselves have seen so much, the walls soaked in it all, witnesses to rebellions great and small, organised and individual. Catholics burning Protestants and Protestants burning Catholics; Lollards and Wycliffites; Recusants and Trinitarians. The deaths of writers, rebels and reformers. The indelible memory of martyrdoms.

A couple of names connect this spot and my journey from Kent. Thomas More signed off many execution orders before Henry VIII demanded his, putting that now-sainted head on a spike: the very head resting in a vault of St Dunstan's church in Canterbury. Wat Tyler lost his head right here, his Peasants' Revolt finally quashed after riding from the pub in Dartford that I passed.

A Scottish Saltire flag and bunches of flowers mark the site where the rebel William Wallace was hanged, drawn and quartered. Anne Askew, twenty-four years old, burned for heresy here: her offence was religious zeal and a rejection of male authority. Anne was carried to the stake on a chair, her joints still dislocated from the Tower rack, a torture session so profound that the Constable of the Tower refused to participate.

Hobbling. Breaking. Burning. Sacrifices based on divine faith or human justice. Punishments meted out by the same logic. Grumbling over sore feet seems laughable.

I'm taking the quiet back streets, keeping parallel with the A1. Through the narrow Cloth Fair, named after the notorious Bartholomew's Fair, swollen from its original purpose as a trade event. From here, the sideshows and stalls gained ground, spilling out into the surrounding parishes and growing increasingly spectacular until the fair became a byword for the sham and vulgar, a magnet for pickpockets and prostitutes. Given the violent entertainments of Smithfield, the lure of caged tigers, performing bears and freak shows come as no surprise. I pause for a hamstring stretch by The Charterhouse, taking in the stately crests and chimneys, arched windows and patchwork walls. Tourists dot the small, park-like centre of the square with its neat flowerbeds, its quiet sense of continuity.

It's pacific here, away from the aura of Smithfield, the din of the fair long diminished. But these walls have seen plenty of turmoil too, shifting in use from priory to Tudor mansion to cloistered hospital and public school; dependent, like faith and gospel truth, upon the whims of State and rule.

I brace myself for a stretch of A1 along Goswell Road, but here, beyond the Barbican, the quiet is sudden, as if the rest of the city has just fallen off a shelf and taken with it all noise and busyness. A man passes by on the corner of Pear Tree Street, his distant cough an audible, echoing bark. There's a separateness to the stretch towards Islington, a sense of stasis. Small pockets of sound pop and dissolve between the bus stops and glassy reception foyers. A carpet of afternoon quiet, of mid-week out-of-window staring; the countdown to August holidays; the prospect of a tea break. Islington is a caffeinated contrast: boutique hipsterdom, gym bodies. The white noise of baristas and moped deliveries. The fizz of harried commerce.

WORKS INCLUDED

Adam Smith, Janet, *Mountain Holidays* (London: J. M. Dent & Sons, 1946)

Atkin, Polly, *Much With Body* (Bridgend: Seren, 2021)

Austen, Jane, *Persuasion* (London: John Murray, 1818)

——, *Pride and Prejudice* (London: T. Egerton, 1813)

Barrett Browning, Elizabeth, *Aurora Leigh: A Poem* (London: J. Miller, 1856)

Beauvoir, Simone de, *The Prime of Life* [*La Force de l'Âge*, 1960], trans. Peter Green (London: Penguin Books, 1960)

Bonner, William Hallam, ed., 'The Journals of Sarah and William Hazlitt, 1822–1831', *University of Buffalo Studies*, XXIV/3 (1959), pp. 172–281

Brontë, Charlotte, *Selected Letters*, ed. Margaret Smith (Oxford: Oxford University Press, 2007)

——, *The Professor* [1857] (Oxford: Oxford University Press, 1998)

Brontë, Emily, *Poems, by Currer, Ellis, and Acton Bell* (London: Aylott & Jones, 1846)

——, *Wuthering Heights* [1847] (London: Penguin, 1994)

——, *Wuthering Heights and Agnes Grey, by Ellis and Acton Bell: A New Edition Revised, with a Biographical Notice of the Authors, a Selection from their Literary Remains, and a Preface*, ed. Currer Bell (London: Smith, Elder and Co, 1850)

Burney, Frances, *Evelina; or, The History of a Young Lady's Entrance into the World* (London: T. Lowndes, 1778)

Chopin, Kate, *The Awakening and Other Stories*, ed. Pamela Knights (Oxford: Oxford University Press, 2008)

Cracknell, Linda, 'Assynt's Rare Animals?', Walkhighlands, www.walkhighlands.co.uk/news/assynts-rare-animals, 8 August 2015

—, *Doubling Back: Ten Paths Trodden in Memory* (Glasgow: Freight Books, 2014)

Davis, Kate, *The Girl Who Forgets How to Walk* (London: Penned in the Margins, 2018)

Dugdale, Sasha, *Deformations* (Manchester: Carcanet Press, 2020)

Dungy, Camille T., *Guidebook to Relative Strangers: Journeys into Race, Motherhood, and History* (New York: W. W. Norton & Company, 2017)

Elkin, Lauren, *Flâneuse: Women Walk the City in Paris, New York, Tokyo, Venice and London* (London: Chatto & Windus, 2016)

Farjeon, Eleanor, *Edward Thomas: The Last Four Years* (Oxford: Oxford University Press, 1958)

Gaffield, Nancy, *Meridian* (Padstow: Longbarrow Press, 2019)

Glover, Merryn, *Of Stone and Sky* (Edinburgh: Polygon, 2021)

Gray, Muriel, *The First Fifty: Munro-Bagging Without a Beard* (London: Corgi, 1991)

Harrison, Melissa, *Rain: Four Walks in English Weather* (London: Faber and Faber, 2016)

Jamie, Kathleen, *Surfacing* (London: Sort Of Books, 2019)

—, *The Queen of Sheba* (Hexham: Bloodaxe Books, 1994)

Keary, Eliza, *Little Seal-Skin, and Other Poems* (London: George Bell and Sons, 1874)

Kesson, Jessie, *Somewhere Beyond: A Jessie Kesson Companion*, ed. Isobel Murray (Edinburgh: B & W Publishing, 2000)

Lawrence, Frieda, *'Not I, But the Wind . . .'* (London: William Heinemann, 1935)

Le Faye, Deirdre, *Jane Austen's Letters* (Oxford: Oxford University Press, 2014)

Lewis, Gwyneth, *Sparrow Tree* (Tarset: Bloodaxe, 2011)

Lloyd-Morgan, Ceridwen, *Letters and Notebooks: Selected from the Gwen John Papers at the National Library of Wales* (London: Tate Publishing with National Library of Wales, 2004)

Mansfield, Katherine, *Journal of Katherine Mansfield* (London: Constable, 1927)

Martineau, Harriet, *A Complete Guide to the English Lakes* (London: Whittaker & Co., 1854)

—, *A Year at Ambleside* (Philadelphia, PA: Sartain's Union Magazine, 1855)

—, *Autobiography* (Boston: James R. Osgood and Company, 1877)

May, Katherine, *The Electricity of Every Living Thing: A Woman's Walk in the Wild to Find Her Way Home* (London: Trapeze, 2018)

Mort, Helen, *No Map Could Show Them* (London: Chatto & Windus, 2016)

Moss, Sarah, *The Fell* (London: Picador, 2021)

Murray, Sarah, *A Companion, and Useful Guide to the Beauties of Scotland* (London: George Nicol, 1799)

Nimmo, Jenny, *The Snow Spider* (London: Methuen, 1986)

Nin, Anaïs, *Under a Glass Bell* (New York: Gemor Press, 1944)

Oswald, Alice, *Woods, etc.* (London: Faber and Faber, 2005)

Overall, Sonia, *Heavy Time* (London: Penned in the Margins, 2021)

Pennington, Montagu, *Memoirs of the Life of Mrs. Elizabeth Carter* (Boston, MA: Oliver C. Greenleaf, 1809)

Rossetti, Christina, *The Complete Poems of Christina Rossetti*, ed. R. W. Crump (London: Penguin, 2005)

Sayers, Dorothy L., *Have His Carcase* (London: Victor Gollancz, 1932)

Sethi, Anita, *I Belong Here: A Journey Along the Backbone of Britain* (London: Bloomsbury, 2021)

Shelley, Mary, *Frankenstein; or, The Modern Prometheus* (London: Lackington, Hughes, Harding, Mavor, & Jones, 1818)

—, *History of a Six Weeks' Tour through a Part of France, Switzerland, Germany and Holland* (London: T. Hookham, 1817)

Shepherd, Nan, *In the Cairngorms* (Edinburgh and London: Moray Press, 1934)

—, *The Living Mountain* [1977] (Edinburgh: Canongate Books, 2011)

Smith, Charlotte, *Rural Walks: In Dialogues: Intended for the Use of Young Persons* (London: T. Cadell, 1795)

Stewart, Alexandra, *Daughters of the Glen*, ed. Innis Macbeath (Aberfeldy: Leura Press, 1986)

Strayed, Cheryl, *Wild: A Journey from Lost to Found* (London: Atlantic Books, 2012)

Thompson, Flora, *Heatherley* [1944] (Hampshire: John Owen Smith, 1988)

—, *Lark Rise to Candleford* [1945] (London: Penguin, 2008)

Vyvyan, C. C., *Down the Rhone on Foot* (London: Peter Owen, 1955)

Wardle, Ralph, ed., *Godwin and Mary: Letters of William Godwin and Mary Wollstonecraft* (Lawrence, KS, and London: University of Kansas Press and Constable & Company, 1967)

Warner, Sylvia Townsend, *Summer Will Show* (London: Chatto & Windus, 1936)

Weeton, Ellen, *Miss Weeton's Journal of a Governess* (Newton Abbott: David & Charles, 1969)

Williams, Helen Maria, *Letters Written in France*, ed. Neil Fraistat and Susan S. Lanser (Peterborough: Broadview Press, 2001)

Winn, Raynor, *The Salt Path* (London: Michael Joseph, 2018)

Woolf, Virginia, *Mrs Dalloway* (London: Hogarth Press, 1925)

—, *Street Haunting: A London Adventure* [1927] (San Francisco, CA: West Gate, 1930)

—, *The Diary of Virginia Woolf*, vol 1: *1931–1935*, ed. Anne Oliver Bell and Andrew McNeillie (London: The Hogarth Press, 1982)

—, *To the Lighthouse* [1927] (Hertfordshire: Wordsworth Editions, 2002)

Wordsworth, Dorothy, *The Grasmere and Alfoxden Journals*, ed. Pamela Woof (Oxford: Oxford University Press, 2002)

—, *The Letters of William and Dorothy Wordsworth: The Middle Years, Part II, 1812–1820*, ed. Ernest de Selincourt (Oxford: Clarendon Press, 1970)

Yearsley, Ann, *Selected Poems* (London: T. Cadell, 1785)

PERMISSIONS

The author and publishers wish to thank the organizations and individuals listed below for authorizing reproductions of their work. Every effort has been made to contact copyright holders; should there be any we have been unable to reach or to whom inaccurate acknowledgements have been made please contact the publishers, and full adjustments will be made to subsequent printings.

From *Brick Lane* by Monica Ali, published by Doubleday. Copyright © 2003, Monica Ali. Reprinted by permission of The Random House Group Limited.

Polly Atkin, 'Unwalking', reproduced by permission of Poetry Wales Press Limited.

Simone de Beauvoir, *La Force de l'âge*, © Editions Gallimard, Paris, 1960.

'Assynt's Rare Animals' and *Doubling Back*, reproduced by permission of Linda Cracknell.

Kate Davis, 'She Teaches Herself to Walk', from *The Girl Who Forgets How to Walk*, reproduced by permission of Penned in the Margins Ltd.

'The Fall of the Rebel Angels', from *Deformations* by Sasha Dugdale is reprinted by kind permission of Carcanet Press, Manchester, UK.

'A Good Hike', from *Guidebook to Relative Strangers: Journeys into Race, Motherhood, and History* by Camille T. Dungy. Copyright © 2017 by Camille T. Dungy. Used by permission of W. W. Norton & Company, Inc.

Flâneuse, reproduced by permission of Lauren Elkin.

Edward Thomas: The Last Four Years by Eleanor Farjeon (Faber & Faber), reproduced by permission of David Higham Associates.

Nancy Gaffield, *Meridian*, reproduced by permission of Longbarrow Press.

ACKNOWLEDGEMENTS

I am very grateful to the National Library of Scotland, Edinburgh, for having such a wonderful collection of writing by women about walking. I have spent many happy days over the last few months reading extraordinary writing by women about their adventures. Paula Williams, curator of map, mountaineering and polar collections, has been a particular help, and it was in part her wonderful exhibition 'Petticoats and Pinnacles', shown at the NLS during 2021 and 2022, that provided the impetus for this project. To all of the staff at the NLS, my sincere thanks.

I am grateful also to the team at Reaktion for their support, from commissioning to publication. David Hayden has been a tremendous help as I navigated the murky waters of permissions and his championing of the book has meant a great deal. Dave Watkins commissioned this project and, although he is no longer at Reaktion, continues to help me keep the faith. I am grateful for his friendship.

I am also grateful to all those on Twitter who shared their favourite literary walks when this project was in its infancy.

The index has been produced by Alison Duncan, whose attention to detail adds so much to the texts she works on. Thank you.

INDEX